THE AUTHOR

Geoff Lee was born in St Helens in early September, 1939, on the first full day of the war, but it is believed that this was just a coincidence. He lived in Lancashire for the first part of his life, but has lived in Yorkshire since 1972. He first worked at Prescot for BICC (British Insulated Callender's Cables), but often referred to locally as the Biggest Individual Collection of Comedians. Since then he has worked in many drawing offices, the source of much of the content of this novel. He is a leading member of the Rugby League Supporters' Association and is responsible for the distribution of its magazine, *'The Greatest Game'*.

One Winter

Romance, Rock 'n' Roll and Rugby League

in the Swinging Sixties

by Geoff Lee

The Parrs Wood Press
Manchester

First Published in 1999

THE PARRS WOOD PRESS
St Wilfrid's Enterprise Centre,
Royce Road, Manchester, M15 5BJ

© Geoff Lee 1999

ISBN: 1 903158 01 X

Printed by:

Fretwell Print and Design
Healey Works
Golbourne Street
Keighley
West Yorkshire BD21 1PZ

ACKNOWLEDGEMENTS

This novel is dedicated to the cast of thousands, those many individuals and characters who it has been good to know, to know about or to hear talking, at work, at the match, in the pub or on the bus. It is mainly from their experiences and tales, plus a few of my own, that this novel has been written.

And if you recognise yourself or bits of yourself in these pages, old friend, then I hope that my portrayal of you is as accurate as most of my drawings were. But if you don't like the way I have described you, or if you think that I have shown you as a boring, miserable old fool, then I am sorry to tell you the bad news. It will be even worse in the next one!

Many people helped me write this book; by telling me their own experiences in life, by recounting funny stories of things that they had seen or done or heard about, but in most cases by just being themselves.

However, a number do deserve a special thanks: Linda Hodgson, who ten years ago typed the first drafts of what was then called 'Tales of a Northern Draughtsman' when I was still operating at the technological level of the biro; Alex Service, the Saints' historian, who provided all the statistics of the 1962/ 63 season; Michael Wray, who led me eventually to The Parrs Wood Press after I had been rejected by just about every other publisher in the land; Andy Searle of The Parrs Wood Press, who has seen the book through to publication with enthusiasm and dedication; and Michael Steele for permission to use his superb photograph on the cover.

Contents

1
THE PETITION

"Would you like to sign this petition? It's to stop them shutting the station."

If he had said that once, he must have said it over a hundred times on that first night.

"I think it's disgraceful. They've only just had it painted."

"I bet Lord Beeching doesn't have to go on the train. I bet he gets driven round in a big posh car."

"Them M.P.'s in London don't care one bit about folk like us."

These comments were typical of what the people of Ashurst thought about the whole business. Almost without fail they would look briefly at the words on his petition and sign. Sometimes it would be taken indoors for more of the family to add their names.

One man asked if his children could sign, or did they have to be twenty one. Another asked if he could put his mother's name down even though she had been dead for over a month.

"She would have signed it, if she had still been with us," he said quietly.

Of course he heard a few daft comments like 'I'll not be able to get to work. I'll have to go on the bus' and 'I don't know. I'll have to wait until my husband comes home'. But at most houses he was well received. Some talked at length about the issue, a few asked him in and one old lady even persuaded him to stay for a cup of tea and some cake she had just baked. Many wished him all the best. He could tell that the way they spoke to him, they fully agreed with what he was doing.

But at work all that the rest of the drawing office wanted to do was make funny comments about his evening activities.

"I think he's training to be a Jehovah's Witness," laughed Charlie, the office comedian.

"Well one thing is for certain," replied Yorky, who always had to get the last word in. "He'll never get into the Mormons if he carries on wearing that dirty old donkey jacket."

Any one listening to them talk might easily have concluded that Wilkinson's draughtsmen were a right cynical lot.

"Greeno's got as much chance of keeping that station open as Mick has of keeping his eyes open this afternoon" and "He's used more pencils on that petition than he's used on his drawing board since he's been here."

The way they liked to have a go at him was partly because he was the youngest and newest amongst them. It was also because he tended to be a bit gullible, something that Charlie had soon picked up on. And some of it was simply his own fault. A typical example had been that business at Salford Technical College.

The firm had sent him there to a course on Electrical Control Systems. Due to the shortage of space, some classes had to be held in houses dotted around the area. At the reception desk in the main building he was told that he would have to go to eight Irlam street, about ten minutes walk away. When he arrived there he walked straight into the house and much to his suprise saw an old woman in a dressing gown sat in front of an electric fire with her hair in curlers toasting a slice of bread.

As this strange young man suddenly burst into her front room, she jumped up, pointed the toasting fork at him and said:

"What do you think you want, lad?"

"Is this Salford Technical College?"

"Does it look like it? It's eight Irlam street, you silly fool."

He muttered an apology and quickly left. As he came back on to the street he saw a large wooden building on the waste ground opposite. It was the Irlam street annexe of Salford Technical College, rooms one to eight. He had obviously made a mistake.

But a bigger mistake was to tell them about it when he arrived back in work the following day. They just went on and on about it, reminding him frequently that many a fine tune could be played on an old fiddle. But it was all good natured and helped the day go along that little bit quicker, not that it could ever be said to be boring at the Wilkinson Engineering Works. This was a place where something was always happening, humorous, dramatic or just plain daft.

When he had first become involved in the campaign to keep the station open, it was suggested that he went out with one of the more experienced campaigners. It seemed a good idea since he had never done this sort of thing before. But he knew how boring it would be if he got lumbered with the likes of Councillor Frodsham, whose main aim in life, now that he had retired, was to become the Mayor of Ashurst.

It would probably be just as bad if he went with Harold Murray. He had fought and been wounded in the Spanish Civil War and never missed a chance to talk about what he had seen and done. It was not that Alan did not respect him. He was well known in the town for his strong principles, and when Fascism had begun to rear its ugly head in the Thirties, he had been prepared to risk his life for what he believed in. But the trouble with Harold was that he always assumed that whoever he was talking to was as interested in the war against Franco as he had been.

2

So he decided to go on his own. He started off in Shaley Brow where many miners lived. Ashurst itself was located right at the centre of the South Lancashire coalfield. Before the War, there had been a dozen pits within the town's boundaries. Now only Havanna, Bank Top and Gillarsfield were still working and many had to travel further afield to other collieries, Parkside at Newton, Bold and Sutton Manor on the edge of St.Helens and Cronton near Widnes.

He had always liked going round Shaley Brow. It was partly because his Auntie Kitty and Uncle Billy once lived there. He remembered again how whenever he walked into their little house in Albion street he would find her reading the Ashurst Weekly Reporter. It never seemed to matter which day of the week it was. As soon as she saw him she would put it down and after reaching up to kiss him on the cheek would say something like, "You've just missed him, he's on two ten" or "He'll be up soon, he's on ten six this week".

Then she would put the kettle on and ask if he was hungry. As long as he could remember she had always had a pan simmering away on the stove. Then, while he was eating, she would sit opposite him and want to know all his news. Sadly, neither of their names would be added to his petition. The previous October, his uncle had gone down with pneumonia. Never a strong man, the years spent loading railway wagons in Hilton's draughty warehouse had finally taken their toll. Confined to his bed, he spent the next three months slowly wasting away. At his funeral Alan thought to himself that his auntie would not long be a widow. She wasn't. Within a month she had also died, gone she would believe to a better place where her Billy would not have to work shifts.

He started in Potter Street. Within an hour he had collected over fifty signatures. He was suprised to find how easy it was, particularly when at number sixteen a man wearing a boiler suit asked him for some blank sheets. "I work at the Cable works in Leigh. I can pass these round the lads on our shift. Call back next week but don't come before half seven."

He carried on until he had passed the hundred mark. By now it was getting dark and he could see the number five trolley bus slowly working its way up Newton Hill. On the journey back into town he asked two women who he heard talking about railways to sign. He assumed that it must be about the closure of the station, or even the campaign itself. However, the subject of their conversation was a Hornby train set one had just bought her son for his birthday. They laughed when they realised his mistake, but still added their names, as did four other passengers and the conductress.

Pleased with his first night's work he decided to go again the following night. He was well on the way to reaching Monday's tally when he knocked on number seven Barton street. A voice shouted out, "Come in, it's open. " As soon as Alan walked in

3

the house he recognised the man sat there. It was Joe Singleton, one of his boyhood heroes.

It was while he had been in Mrs. Duxberry's class that he had started watching the Saints. Going to the match soon became their main event of the week. He and his friends would first catch the bus into St. Helens. There they would join the queue for the football specials. Sometimes there were supporters from the away team on it, and as the bus made its way down Duke Street and along Boundary Road Alan would listen to all the banter, particularly when the away team was from over the Pennines and the old rivalry between Lancashire and Yorkshire surfaced once again.

They always tried to get inside the boys' pen early so they could stand right at the front. Shortly before the kick off, a boy not much bigger than them walked round the ground carrying a blackboard on which the changes to the programme were chalked. Shortly after, the crowd at the Eccleston end would begin cheering. They were the first to see the players as they came out of the tunnel. Usually the Saints ran out first wearing their white shirts with a red band, white shorts and red and white socks. After that came the away team and then the referee and the touch judges, usually greeted by booing and ribald comments from around the ground.

Like all small boys, Alan had his favourites. Len Aston, the captain; his friend Ronnie actually knew him! They used to live in the same street until they had moved to Ashurst when he was seven. Joe Ball was another; he played at full back and worked at the United Glass Bottle works at Sherdley with his Uncle Jack. Then there were the Stott brothers, Jimmy and Tommy, his namesake Duggie Greenall, Max Garbler the Australian, Jimmy Honey, Peter Metcalfe, Todder Dickinson, Alan Prescot and more.

Joe was not a first teamer, but Alan had always liked to watch him play. He had a good side step, but as those who knew what they were talking about said of him, he couldn't tackle.

"I remember you scoring a hat trick against Liverpool Stanley."

"That must have been a long time ago."

"It was. I was only nine."

"Ee. Happy days."

They talked briefly about the current Saints team and then the conversation moved back to the campaign. Finally, as Alan turned to leave his one time hero said: "Do you know who lives opposite. Ernie Bradshaw."

Ernie was a Rugby League star from before the War. Alan had obviously never seen him play but had heard a lot about him. It made him realise that as he went round with the petition, he would no doubt meet other players and former stars.

Ashurst did not have its own team but it was still very much a Rugby League town, though with split loyalties due to its geographical location. The majority followed the Saints, but those who lived up Nook End were more likely to follow Wigan.

He moved on to Hope Street where at number five he met Ken Finney, a friend of his brother Paul. Next door he was invited in by a woman to meet her father, who was old enough to remember the station being built.

Tales from the past had always interested Alan. It was something he had picked up from his grandparents. His grandad, Ned Holding, loved to talk about the days when he was at school and then when he first started work down the pit. He also had a fine collection of stories about the War. He had been one of the first men in the town to volunteer. Strangely enough he saw little fighting, he was captured early in 1915 and spent the next three years working down a lead mine in Prussia. It was during this period of his life that he developed an interest in foreign languages and foreign countries, something which he had passed on to his youngest grandchild.

It was from his grandmother that Alan had picked up his interest in local history. Almost all her life had been spent within the boundaries of the town except for the odd day trip in summer to New Brighton or Southport. Even after she was married, a visit to St Helens was considered a bit special while a shopping trip to Liverpool was an event to be planned weeks ahead and talked about endlessly afterwards.

So when old man Aspinall began talking about the early days of the railway, Alan listened with great interest. Unfortunately he had a morbid way of telling his tales, dwelling on the many deaths and accidents he had seen or knew about. He would have stayed longer, but the man's daughter, who herself must have been at least sixty, asked him to go since her father was getting tired.

"He doesn't talk much about the past. There's never anyone who wants to listen. The only folk who visit him now are the priest and the insurance man and neither are interested. But do come again, he's enjoyed your visit, haven't you Dad?" Then lowering her voice, she said, "But don't stay too long if you do come, he's not that well."

Sadly it was not to be. Two weeks later, Alan read in the Ashurst Reporter that the old man had passed away three days before his ninety second birthday.

He had now collected over two hundred signatures and enjoyed doing it. It was really interesting, meeting people, some of whom he knew well and some whom he only knew by sight but now knew by name. As a result he decided to go again on the Wednesday night.

He started off in Lowton Terrace where he immediately attracted the attention of a large dog, so he moved off into Hesketh Street where at the first house he wasted a long time arguing with a snooty woman who told him that Lord Beeching and Harold MacMillan knew a damn sight more about the state of British Railways than he could ever hope to. He carried on for another hour and was just about ready to call it a day when at the end house in Bolton street the door was opened by Roy Penketh, an electrician who he had worked with as an apprentice.

"Hello, Alan. I didn't know your mum let you stay out so late at night. Tek your clogs off and come in."

Roy now worked for Wilkinson's Outside Contracts Division and was frequently out of town. As a result he knew little about the campaign. He listened while Alan briefly told him the details, and then, after he and his wife had signed his sheet, he said: "It's nearly dark. You can't go knocking on doors now or you'll get locked up. Why don't you come for a pint?"

They had never had a petition in The Lamb before and it caused quite a stir as Roy began to pass it round pointing to Alan as he did so. Soon the regulars began treating him like a bit of a celebrity. They would come to the bar where he and Roy were stood and buy both them a drink. After all the talking and walking round the streets, he really needed it. He must have had at least four pints and they soon had an effect on what was now a very tired body. As a result he didn't remember much of what happened after the third one had gone down. But he did recall an old man with a pipe slapping him on the back as he walked out at the end and saying:

"That was very good lad. I've enjoyed it. Come back tomorrow and we can all sign it again."

2
THE START OF THE CAMPAIGN

"Have tha passed then, owd lad?"

The question was asked by Chris Ashton, a shift engineer at Bold Power Station. They were sat in the Eagle and Child with a few others after having just finished the last exam for their Higher National Certificate.

"I think I have. What about you?"

"I don't know. I cocked the Electrical Technology paper up on Monday neet."

They went over the questions on the paper they had just handed in and compared notes. The first pint soon went down and as they began to organise the next round, Chris looked at his watch and stood up.

"Are you not staying for another?"

"I can't. I was supposed to be at work half an hour ago."

"You'd better go then. We don't want to end up supping in the dark."

"Eh Greeno, if you've passed, will they still keep you on just changing light bulbs?"

It was Neil Churchill, who had been an apprentice with Alan but now worked at Mather's Foundry.

"You're a bit out of touch, Winnie. I've been in the drawing office since April."

"The only thing Greeno ever draws is his wages," said Stan Morris, an electrician in Wilkinson's Rolling Mill.

"I bet you don't know they're going to hang some of my drawings in the Walker Art Gallery."

"They must have run out of bog paper then."

They began talking about what they were going to do with all the spare time they now had at their disposal. The pub had a new landlord and the beer had certainly improved since the last time he had been in there, even if the decor hadn't. And he also knew he could come again any night he wanted to, although it wouldn't be quite the same, even if all the rest of them turned up again.

It finally hit him that it really was all over as he sat eating his tea the following night. And as he ate, he watched Mr. Astbury, their next door neighbour, watering his lettuces.

"So where are you off tonight?" asked his mum.

"I'm going down to Ken's. We'll probably go for a game of bowls and then up to the Feathers."

"Did you go for a drink last night?"

"Yes, we went to the Eagle."

"I thought you must have. You made enough noise when you came in." Then she went on, "Before you go out, will you put all your books and papers away in a safe place? They'll only get lost if you don't and you'll be blaming me when it comes to signing on again and you can't find them."

As soon as he had finished his tea, he went upstairs and did what she had asked. He looked at the previous night's exam paper, then put it inside his Principles of Electrical Engineering. He must have opened that book every day for the last three months. He wondered if he would ever open it again.

He sat on his bed and looked out of the window. From there he had a panoramic view of the town. To the south he could see the winding gear of the Havanna colliery. To the right but nearer was Wardle's bakery and Ashurst Parish church, now partly obscured by the school they were building in Hall Lane. In the centre of his view a mile away was his old school, Lane Head Juniors. In the distance were the cooling towers of Bold Power Station. To the right he could see the distinctive frontage of the Rivoli cinema and behind it Mather's Foundry.

In the foreground were the gardens of their neighbours and those in Martin Lane that ran at right angles to Chisnall Avenue. He noticed that Mr. Astbury was now digging up a corner of the lawn he had so painstakingly laid last year. Short of an earthquake or a typhoon, he would be there until it was pitch black. Never did a man spend so much time on such a small piece of land. He watched the smoke from a train waft across his view. He waited until the last traces had disappeared. Then he went downstairs, rubbed Brylcreem in his hair, combed it like Tony Curtis and shouted goodbye to his Mum, who was now talking to Mrs Astbury.

He walked down Parry Lane where he chatted to an old miner. He was always sat in his front garden whenever Alan went past, catching up on all the sunshine he had missed while working for years in the bowels of the earth. He turned into Seddon Avenue and kicked a ball about with a couple of young lads before finishing up at number six.

As he was let into the house, Alan could hear an almighty row going on in the back. Before he could ask about it, Ken said: "Have you heard the news? Beeching is trying to close the station and the branch line up to Leigh."

"And has the noble Lord come to tell your Dad to his face."

8

"No, it's Brother Bradley, the union man from Liverpool. He's bloody useless. My dad can't stand him."

A few minutes later the heated exchanges came to an end and, as soon as his unwelcome visitor had left, Arthur Parr came into the front room.

"Hello, Alan. Long time no see. I thought you must have emigrated or started courting or summat."

"No. I've been doing my exams. I only finished last night. Anyway, what's this about the station?"

But before Ken's Dad could reply, there was a knock on the door. "Are you ready Arthur?" the two lads heard the Parr's next door neighbour, Len Atherton, ask.

"I'll just nip upstairs and have a wash. I've only just got rid of Buggerlugs Bradley. Give us five minutes. Go in the front room, our Ken's in there."

"How are you doing Alan? I've not seen you for ages. I thought you'd stopped coming down the poor end of town!" Then he went on, "I suppose you've heard they're trying to shut the station? Bloody Government!"

"Yes. I've just heard."

"There's a meeting about it at the cricket club tonight. Are you coming?"

"I don't know anything about it, Len."

"It doesn't matter. Neither does anybody else. And it's a good pint in there."

"Well, I suppose so."

Alan hadn't really banked on sitting in a meeting on his first night of freedom. But then he could hardly say no, not if it involved anything to do with Ken's dad.

As soon as they had settled down in the lounge of the Ashurst Cricket and Social Club, the club chairman Jim Delaney called them to order.

"You'll have all heard the news that they want to close the station. A few of us at work thought it would be a good idea to have a meeting about it. Because it's such short notice, there will be a lot of folk who aren't here who should be, so this will have to be something to get things started." He made a few general comments and then threw it open for discussion.

The first to speak was Joe Day, who immediately began to talk about what his union, the National Union of Railwaymen, had to do. But before he could say much he was interrupted by an old man at the back of the room. As soon as Alan saw him, he guessed he had once been a collier. It was the way he stood, the way he made his point.

"We've had it if that bugger Bradley gets involved in it. We all know what he's like. He'll be wanting minutes for every meeting, seven days notice for any action, and we'll spend half the time discussing a constitution and how many for a quorum. I'm sorry, Joe but the less we have to do with that man the better."

The next speaker was Bill Martindale, a crane driver at Mathers, who proceeded to give a long rambling account of why the railways had been nationalised in the first place.

He was followed by John Taylor, who worked in the Town Hall. He was a real wet blanket. In his view nothing would stop the Government closing the station if it wanted to. Their only hope lay in Hugh Gaitskell and the Labour Party winning the next General Election. His contribution was about as useful as a chocolate fireguard. It was not quite clear why he had turned up, unless his wife had sent him.

"Well, if you take that attitude, we might as well pack up now." It was Bill Sephton, an electrician at Jarratts and well known for his left wing views. "But in my view, if we get a campaign going with a lot of people in it, we can soon make them change their minds. It won't be the first time that Beeching has had his plans squashed."

A few more asked questions or made general comments and then up stood Mr. Donaldson, the local expert on railway matters. According to him there were certain bye-laws in existence that prevented the station's function being changed except by an Act of Parliament. It was something to do with the problems that had arisen when it had been built in 1882. He offered to look into it and see if they could use them to their advantage.

By now the meeting had been going on for well over an hour, and one or two indicated that they would soon have to leave. Knowing there was little more to be gained by dragging it on, the chairman proposed that they bring things to a halt by agreeing some basic points.

"Firstly, all those present want to keep the station open - agreed." Every one nodded or said aye. "Secondly, we need a campaign that will involve as many people as possible - agreed." Again there was general support for his suggestion.

"Can we not get a petition up?"

"Are you proposing that, Horace?"

"Aye"

"I'll second that." It was Mrs. Jaundrill, who had the newspaper shop in Cambridge Street, "and I'll put a poster in my window if we get some."

"Well, if we are going to have a petition , we'll have to do it properly." It was John Taylor again. He coughed importantly and then said, "I suggest something like this: 'We humble and loyal servants of your gracious Majesty humbly beseech you to use your honourable position to urge your Ministers of the Crown to intercede on our behalf and keep open Ashurst station.'"

"It's not a bloody court circular we want. Let's have it in plain English that folk can understand." It was Harry Cheetham, a Labour councillor. "I propose the following: We, the residents of Ashurst, object strongly to the proposal by Lord Beeching to close Ashurst railway station and the Leigh branch line."

"Just a minute," a bus driver, still wearing his uniform, said, "Only people who live in Ashurst can sign that. I propose it be changed to something lik,e "We, the residents of Ashurst and members of the travelling public object strongly to the proposal to close Ashurst station and the Leigh branch line."

"That's better," said Arthur "but it needs some bite. Let's add the words, and will use all in our power to prevent it."

"If you are going to say that you must say, all in our legal power. We don't want to go breaking the law do we." The speaker was, not suprisingly, Mr Donaldson, the legal expert.

Not wishing to provoke any antagonism, Arthur suggested: "We, the people of Ashurst and members of the general public, object strongly to the proposed closure of Ashurst station. We promise to do all that is legally and morally necessary to prevent it."

At this, everyone in the room shouted their approval and, before Mr Donaldson could raise the thorny question of what happens when morality clashes with legality, the chairman announced it was clearly acceptable to all present. He then suggested that they should soon have another meeting when they could elect a committee and decide what to do next.

As soon as the meeting finished, a man who hadn't spoken limped up to Arthur. He was a printer and told Arthur that he could get some petition sheets done at work. So Arthur proceeded to write out with a little embellishment what he had just said.

"We, the people of Ashurst and the surrounding areas of South Lancashire, object strongly to the proposals of Lord Beeching to close down Ashurst station and the Ashurst to Leigh branch line. We promise to do all that is legally and morally necessary to prevent it." He read it out loud. It seemed all right he thought. But before he could think of anything better, the printer had taken it from him.

"Sorry Arthur, I'll have to go or I'll miss the bus."

So in that way the petition against the closure of Ashurst railway station and the branch line to Leigh came into being.

3
EARLY DAYS 1939 – 1955

Robert Alan Greenall was born on the first day of September 1939. Before he could be brought home to number thirty two Chisnall Avenue and the eager clutches of his eight year old brother Paul and five year old sister Joan, the storm clouds that had been brewing over Europe for months finally broke. Around the very time he was being delivered in Victoria Hospital, Hitler's troops were marching into Poland, and within two days the Second World War had started.

As a small boy he frequently heard the air raid sirens and the drone of aircraft overhead at night. He remembered the windows being blacked out, carrying his gas mask round in a cardboard box, and standing in endless queues with his mother. Around the age of five he remembered watching a bonfire in Fairclough's field, where he would later go pea picking. He couldn't understand why someone had put a picture of a man with a moustache on the top of it. It looked just like his Uncle Albert.

It wasn't long after that soldiers were seen around the town. Slowly he began to understand that no man in a khaki uniform would be coming to their house to lift him up in the air and give him presents from his bag. His own father, Arthur John Greenall, had been called up in January 1940. Except for one short visit he made to see his wife and three young children, he never saw Lancashire again. He died from injuries received in bitter fighting around Monte Casino, one of over a hundred thousand allied troops killed or wounded in the liberation of Italy.

Despite this loss, Alan enjoyed his childhood. He had many relatives, most of whom lived within walking distance of their house. There were lots of children around as well and with them Alan would do all the things boys did in those early days after the war. Most evenings would be spent playing football or cricket on the back fields, marbles in the road, building dens on Wallwork's tip and later on, when they acquired their own transport, cycle speedway and hide and seek on bikes.

Collecting various items took up an enormous amount of their time. This basically took two forms. Firstly, there were things they could physically handle such as football programmes, stamps, Gillick cards, birds' eggs and cigarette packets. This last one usually involved going to the many slag heaps that were dotted all over the town. Oblivious to the dangers to life and limb, they would also dig up all sorts of interesting rubbish and bits of machinery that they would find some passing use for.

The other form of collecting, more accurately described as spotting car registration numbers, was a particular craze for a long time. The way this worked was as follows: each one had to keep his eye out for a car or lorry with the registration number one, ADJ 1 or BEK 1 for example. When he had seen it, he could move on to two, then three and so on. It was a game taken very much on trust, all you had to do was tell the others whenever you had been successful. It would have been very easy to cheat, but pointless since there was no actual end to the game. It just carried on and on until it petered out.

After a while they began spotting BRS lorries. This didn't last long, and around the time he was eleven it was replaced by trainspotting, something he carried on with for years after.

Reading comics was another of his pastimes. He had the Radio Fun bought for him every week by Auntie Doris. It was always on the table when he came in from school on Thursday along with a thre'penny bit for his spends. Then, by swapping over the course of the next seven days, he would also read Adventure, Hotspur, Wizard and Rover. The system worked like clockwork until someone went away for a week's holiday or fell ill. When Geoff Platt was taken to Whiston isolation hospital with scarlet fever, chaos reigned in their reading patterns for weeks.

Another thing he enjoyed was listening to the wireless. The first programme he could remember was Children's Hour and its signature tune Greensleeves. They always had it on, just as his mum was putting their tea on the table. It was the only time there was ever complete silence in the house. He also liked to listen to Jimmy Jewel and Ben Warris in Up The Pole, Tommy Handley in ITMA, Arthur Askey, Ted Lune and the Wednesday night show from the Hippodrome with Enoch, Ramsbottom and Me. But the best programme of them all, without doubt, was Dick Barton Special Agent. Even in the middle of some big game they would all rush home to listen to the adventures of Dick, Jock and Snowy.

All this took place while he was at Lane Head Junior school. It was a time when the sun shone every day in the summer and the snow was over six feet deep in the winter. It was a time when he never had a care in the world, a time when he could go for days without a penny in his pocket and it didn't matter. He always had something to do and something to look forward to. But when Miss Welsby told them on their last day that they had been a pleasure to teach, it began to sink in that they had come to the end of a very special period in their lives.

A few of his class passed the scholarship, but he was the only one to go to Ashurst grammar school. It was not something that he could say that he enjoyed. But in 1955, on May the ninth, it no longer mattered. That was the day he heard that he was to become an apprentice. And ten weeks later, as he sat on the bus taking him to

Wilkinson's Engineering works on his first day, that all could be forgotten. He looked round the smoke filled upper deck and guessed that most of the passengers would be going to the same place. He was right. As it turned into Aspinall Street, they rose, almost as one. The conductor shouted out Butlins. No body laughed. He always did it.

He walked passed the General Offices and down to the Apprentice School where about twenty other young men, some of whom he already knew, were stood about. There they were greeted by a man wearing a flat cap and a white smock.

"Morning, lads. I'm Jack Critchley, the apprentice Training Officer. Now I know it has been said many times, but today really is the first day in the rest of your life. You are now at work and I want you to start off as you intend to continue so I am going to begin by introducing you to Critchley's Three Golden Rules."

He walked to the far end of the room, opened a window and went on. "The first one is to do with time-keeping. We start at eight. To show you are here you have to clock on. If you clock on one minute late, you will get quartered. That means you will lose a quarter of an hour's pay. Dinner hour is twelve till one, you clock out at twelve, and you clock on before one and you clock off at ten past five.

"The second rule is to do with safety. I've been here over twenty years and I've seen some bad accidents in that time. The worse one was a young apprentice, not much older than any of you. He thought he was clever taking a short cut across the rolling mill floor to get to the canteen. He thought the shift had finished. Well it hadn't, the last bar was slow coming through. It took two months before he finally died. It was terrible. He was burned all over. Any one breaking any of the safety rules gets sent home for the rest of the week and that means no pay.

"The third Golden Rule is to remember that you are here to learn a trade. The men you will be working with are all experts in their own way, well most of them. They can teach you a lot, but they will only do so if you show them that you want to learn. And if you don't want to learn, then there's the door so you might as well go home now.

"These rules are very simple. I've got a few more. In fact I've got a lot more, but we'll start off with these. You can remember them as the three B's. Be here on time. Be safety conscious. Be prepared to learn. And you forget them at your peril.

"As regards your wages, you get paid on Friday morning. From your top line there are some deductions, Income Tax and National Insurance stamp and a penny for the Social Club. In September you will be going to the technical college one day and one night a week. You get paid for the day you go. It's just like being at work. You don't get paid if you don't go and I will want to know why.

"Then there's the matter of joining the union. You don't have to join until you have come out of your time. But there are a number of benefits, and if you join straightaway you'll get on a lot better with the men you are working with. It also depends on where you are. The electricians are red hot. They call the Electrician's shop, the Kremlin. The Machine shop lads are pretty keen too. The branch secretary works in there. The plumbers aren't too bothered until you are eighteen. The tin bashers and joiners, they are pretty easy going as well. Anyway that's up to you."

He then spent the next hour talking about the company, its products and what was expected of the apprentices. Then he asked if any of them had any questions. A few did and, while he was telling them about the various sports facilities they could use, in walked two young men in overalls.

"Are these the lambs for the slaughter?" the first one said.

"Oh, Jimmy. You haven't even washed your hands. Look at them and your face. They're filthy."

"It's not one of your new golden rules is it Jack?" the lad replied.

Then the second one chipped in.

"It shows he's been grafting."

"Or it may just be he fell asleep in the sand wash," replied Jack.

The new apprentices could soon sense the camadarie behind this brief encounter. Its shop floor humour was something that Wilkinson's was well known for.

"These two are proof there's life after death. They haunt me. The ugly one is Jimmy Shuttleworth, from the machine shop, and the even uglier one is Dave Bell from the foundry, Wilkinson's own Frankie Lane. They are going to take you round the works. Get back here about half three, will you Jimmy?"

And with that they all filed out to see what the factory they had heard so much about was really like.

As they walked round, they would all recognise many familiar faces; former school friends, neighbours and relatives. One lad saw his dad working on a milling machine, another saw his uncle carrying a ladder. Then, as they stood in the queue in the canteen at lunchtime, one of them pointed towards a young woman serving the chips and said:

"Look at the redhead. She could have me on a plate any day."

"That's my sister," the lad behind him replied.

By the end of the day, Alan had spoken to at least a dozen people. He was particularly pleased to have seen two of his old school friends, Ronnie Harper and Ray Forshaw. He had not seen them for ages. Standing in the bus queue, he saw John Harris, who used to live in Martin Avenue. He was stood with a young woman who looked familiar, possibly Janice Maloney, who had also been in their class.

What had Jack Critchley said about being an apprentice at Wilkinsons; like being at school with money in your pocket. Perhaps it was going to be so in other ways too.

As he ate his tea, he thought about all the things he had seen. Based on his first impressions, he knew that he was going to like it there: the noise, the smells, the machinery, the general atmosphere of the place; all that and he would be earning money as well. He felt sure that he was going to make a lot of new friends there, hopefully among some of the girls who he had seen in the brass foundry. And he was also looking forward to meeting up with some old friends again.

Seeing Ray Forshaw reminded him of those happy days at Lane Head school. For no particular reason he recalled that time he had upset Mrs Walton and then been so embarrassed by her punishment. That had been Ray's fault - Ray owed him one for that. He remembered how they had been sitting at the back of the class during one of her many boring lessons, probably poetry or religion. The two of them had been humming the theme tune of the popular radio programme, Riders of the Range. Suddenly she had called out:

"Who is making all that noise at the back? Is that you Greenall? Come out here at once."

It wasn't really him, it was only half him. In fact, it was less than half him, since Ray was doing it much louder. He was brought to the front of the class and told, "Don't just sing it for Raymond. Sing it for all of us!"

"I can't. I don't know the words."

"Well, sing us one of the songs Miss Travis has taught you in your Music class."

"I can't. I've forgotten them."

"What. All of them."

He looked at the rest of the class. They all had a smile on their faces. He knew that they knew what was going to happen next. Out would come the cane. Never a day went by that Mrs Walton didn't use it or threaten to use it. But his punishment was quite unexpected and far worse.

"Go to Miss Travis now, and ask her to tell you the words of one of her songs and the tune."

With that Alan had to go upstairs to class 4B where Miss Travis was teaching. "Come in," she bellowed as he tapped on the door. He could tell by the sound of her voice that she was not in a good mood. When he told her within earshot of her class, all of whom were a year older than him, why Mrs Walton had sent him, they all burst out laughing. And then when Miss Travis told him to sing the song in front of her own class as well, he just wished the earth would swallow him up.

Wilkinson's might well become like school with money in your pocket, as Jack Critchley had said, but one thing was for sure, he was never going to sing there for anybody.

4
THE DRAWING OFFICE

After working for eighteen months as an electrician, Alan transferred into the Drawing Office. By the end of his first week he knew he had made a good move. The work was interesting and the Electrical Section were a good bunch of men to work with. And just like on the shop floor, there was no end to all the humour and the back chat, particularly between Charlie and Yorky.

Charlie was the office joker. He was a past master at delivering the punch line to his stories and could often tell the same tale over and over again and still get a laugh. He was also a great impersonator and could mimic people from all over the factory, both their voices and their mannerisms. He was always having a go at Yorky and anything to do with that piece of England that lay between the Pennines and the North Sea. Whenever this started, not suprisingly the rest of them always took Charlie's side and invariably, Yorky lost the argument.

Samuel John Holroyd to give him his full name had been brought up on the moors above Halifax. During the war he had served in the Merchant Navy and continued to sail the Seven Seas until he had gone to the wedding of one of his ship mates in Ashurst Parish church. "Going to one wedding often leads to another" the old saying goes and that is just what happened to Sam. He met a widow whose husband had been killed down the pit and within the year was living with his new wife and her young son in her neat little house in Hemsley.

Another lively relationship was between Charlie and Mick. Charlie came from St.Helens. Mick was a Wiganer. Both were keen Rugby League fans, forever arguing over the playing skills and abilities of two of the game's most famous clubs and two of its finest wingers, Tom Van Vollenhoven and Billy Boston.

All the others came from Ashurst. Stan was the oldest. He was fifty two and lived on the edge of town with his sick wife. It ought to have been the other way round if Stan's war record was considered. He had joined up in October 1939, been injured at Dunkirk and later seen action in North Africa. And in 1945 he had taken part in the liberation of Belsen, something he rarely spoke about.

If Stan was the office war hero, Len was its conscience. He was the only one of them to still hold his union card. He was forever trying to convince the others that they should re-join so that they could do something about the things they were always moaning about. But though they usually agreed with him, they never did much about it. It was true that the wages were below the district average, but the conditions were all right and there was always plenty of things to do and talk about other than work.

The sixth member of the electrical section was Dickie. He had moved into the drawing office after he had hurt his back in an accident and been forced to change to a less physical job.

The final member of the section was Tony. He was two years older than Alan and had something of a sadistic streak within him. He was always playing tricks on the others, though he never liked anybody doing the same to him. Not many did, since he was six foot tall and over thirteen stone.

Alan soon noticed how Mick had perfected the art of sleeping while giving the impression he was awake. He would hold his pencil against his board and when any body spoke to him it would move as his left hand went up to the top of his board. Then he'd turn his head as he opened his eyes.

One of Tony's tricks was to crawl under Mick's reference table when he had dozed off and tie his leg to it with a piece of string. Then he would go to another office and ring the electrical section number. Whoever answered it would bawl out "Mick - phone". Mick would then go through the usual procedure and as he began to get down from his stool he would fall to the floor. By the time he had picked himself up, Tony would be back into the office, as always with a big smile on his face.

After Alan had been there a month, the temperature soared up into the eighties. One of the few successes the Staff Association had achieved was to get the firm to provide iced orange juice. The office representative on the committee was Mick. He did it, because he had always done it and because no-one else wanted to. So when it became unbearably hot the others would start pestering him to get the drinks organised.

Normally a couple of the labourers would bring it up in a large open container from the canteen, but on that particular day what happened was that it was sent up in the lift to the first floor where Mick was waiting. As he opened the lift door, he asked Tony, who was walking past, to give him a hand.

Each took hold of a handle with Mick walking backwards. As they walked through the office, Mick slowed down. Tony didn't with the result that some juice slopped over onto Mick. He lifted his end up about half an inch and the juice slopped the other way onto Tony, who then did the same. Suddenly the two were out of synchronisation and juice was slopping from side to side and over the top. Mick tried to put his end down, then lifted it up again, just as Tony, was lowering his end. This resulted in Tony getting drenched. He then tipped his end up, so that more juice slopped over Mick. It only took a few seconds for this to happen, but it was hilarious to watch. Finally enough had been spilled so that they were able to get the thing onto the ground.

18

There was juice all over the place, on Stan's reference table, on the glass cupboard where the drawing office standards were kept and all over the two of them. Mick himself wasn't bothered. He was wearing the old pair of trousers and boots he used when going into the foundry. Tony on the other hand had stains all down his new trousers. It would be advisable to keep out of his way for the rest of the day.

He hated coming off second best. On the other hand he never cared who he upset. Typical was what he had done to Elsie the previous week. Their usual tea lady, Joan was off, so she brought the trolley round. After she had poured out the teas she left it there and went back to the canteen, just like Joan always did. While she was away, Tony pushed it into one of the side offices and covered it with drawings. Elsie was fairly new to Wilkinson's and was quite shy. When she came back and and heard Tony say "You'll get sacked for this. No-one has ever lost a tea trolley before" she almost burst into tears.

The section was completed by Elaine and Anne. Elaine was often called the fastest tracer in the West. Nobody said it to Anne but she was probably the slowest. In charge of them all was Harry Groves, the only manager to come to work on a bike.

One thing Alan soon began to enjoy was the morning tea break discussion. One of them would make a comment about something he had seen on the TV the previous night or read in the paper that morning and then the others would join in. One day Charlie set the ball rolling by referring to a programme on the supernatural that he had watched over the week end.

Then Stan suprised them by stating how he had seen a ghost when he was an apprentice. He was never one to make outlandish statements or say things that he couldn't back up.

"Was that before you started wearing glasses?" smiled Yorky.

Stan shook his head, put down his pipe, leaned back on his stool and began his story.

"I was helping an electrician wire a switch on this big oil tank when I worked at Wallworks. I had to climb up to the top to see what happened when he pressed the start button. When I looked inside there was a man in there. I shouted to him but he ignored me so I climbed down to tell the electrician. Just then the shop foreman came over and asked us what was up."

"There's a man in there."

"What does he look like?"

"He's about fifty, bald head with glasses and wearing an old raincoat," I said.

"You've just seen George Anders. He worked here before the War. He got crushed by one of the rollers they used to have in the old rolling mill. He often comes back around this time of year. Go back up. He'll be gone now."

"He was right. When I climbed back up and looked in the tank, there wasn't a trace of him, but I'll swear on my mother's grave I saw him."

Then it was Yorky's turn.

"I remember when I first went on nights. They had a right big paint mixer at this place I was working at in Halifax. It was a bit like one of these new washing machines with paddles at right angles to each other. When it was full, the motor drove these paddles round and mixed the paint.

"The electrician there was a right little fellow. He was the only one who could get into the thing. As usual he was in a big rush. Go Go they used to call him. He turned the main isolator off first. He should have locked it because it was in the next shop, but he didn't. He thought it would only be a five minute job. Just then the charge hand gets a rush job to do. When he comes out of his office, he noticed the isolator was off, so without thinking he switched it back on. Then his phone rings so he went back to answer it.

"By this time Go Go had crawled back inside the mixer. Suddenly the paddles start to turn as the paint pours over him. He was at the back of it so all he could do was walk round until he was opposite the door and get out quick.

"Now as luck would have it, I was walking through the paint shop to the stores, about midnight it was. It was all dark and quiet and then I heard this whining noise when the motor started up and about six foot in front of me this white flash comes hurtling out towards me. I were terrified. I were sure it were a ghost"

These were typical of their tales. There were tales of things they had seen, things they had done. They were about events at Wilkinson's or other places where they had worked. There were tales from their schooldays, as apprentices, or tales of the scrapes they got into before they were married or in some cases afterwards as well. From time to time they would talk about what they had done in the war or the famous people they had once met or known. It was never ending, there was always one of them with a story to tell, and in addition their many visitors from the shop floor would often chip in with their two penny worth.

Sometimes they were serious but most of the time they had a funny side to them or an unusual twist. Often they seemed a bit far fetched, but then they were all draughtsmen, with their creative ability to present a different perspective on the world in which everybody else lived. And as Charlie said after one particularly rib hurting session:

"Somebody should write a book about all these stories. It'd be a best seller."

At first Alan just listened. Then one morning Frank, one of the old timers, who had called in to see Charlie, told them how he was not even fourteen when he first started work.

20

"That's nothing. I was only eleven when I started."

"Eleven, do you mean mental age," said Yorky.

"No, I was eleven when we went picking peas on Billy Fairclough's fields, up our way. We'd watched these two old women do it. It seemed dead easy, so we asked them first thing one morning if we could do it. They said they were thought it would be all right. They gave us a wicker basket and we went off to the far side of the field and started. After a bit old Billy appeared on his tractor. He spent some time talking to the old biddies. Then he walked over and just as he got near to us, his face dropped. He put his hand in his pocket, gave me a thre'penny bit and told us to piss off."

"What's up, them women said it would be all right for us to pick peas."

"Maybe they did," he said, "but I bet they never told you to chuffing shell'em as well."

Just as Alan was delivering the punch line an electrician walked in to tell Charlie he was needed down in the Rolling Mill. So he could not gauge whether they thought his story was funny, but from then on he was frequently referred to as Pea Brain.

5
THE TRIP TO BLACKPOOL

Every September the Drawing Office ran a trip to Blackpool. It was always a popular event and there were always more that wanted to go than there was room for on the coach. But Alan managed it due to a late and rather amusing withdrawal by Ronnie Garner.

The previous week Big Ron had been on the Machine Shop bowling trip to Oldham where the foreman used to live. In the evening, Ronnie and a couple of the others started chatting to three women in a pub. As time approached last orders he asked one of them if he could he take her home. She was pretty drunk by this time. He definitely heard her say yes and he thought he heard her say that she lived in Leigh. So he took her back to the coach and bang on midnight it left.

On the way down the East Lancashire Road, Ronnie drags himself out of her sleepy embrace and asks the driver to go through Leigh. Then he goes back to Maureen in order to find out exactly where she lived. He could still not get much sense out of her until the coach stopped outside the Town Hall.

"Where are we? I've never been here before," she muttered.

"It's Leigh Town Hall, I thought you said you lived here."

"No. I live in Lees."

"Where's that?"

"In Oldham."

Ronnie's problem now was how to get her home. There was only one way he could do it. He would have to drive her back in his own car. But he would have to do it without his wife knowing. He pushed it out of the garage and down the road until it was out of hearing range, started the engine and then picked up Maureen who he had left at the end of the road.

All the way back, she kept saying, "Can't you go any quicker? I want to be in my bed."

So do I, thought Ronnie.

By four 'o' clock they were back in Oldham, less than a mile from the pub they had been in the previous night.

"Thanks Ronnie. You can drop me off here."

"Can I not come in for a bit?"

"Not now. It's too late. My husband works shifts and he'll be back in half an hour."

When Ronnie arrived back home, he had quite a bit of explaining to do to his wife, so he decided to drop out of the Blackpool trip.

On the coach Alan sat with Keith Sanderson, a draughtsmen from the Mechanical section. From their conversation he soon found out about life in the top half of the office. Physically, the Electrical and Mechanical sections were seperated by the Chief Draughtsman's office and the store room. But this didn't explain why there was never any laughing and joking amongst those who worked in the top half of the drawing office. It was all due to Arthur (You can't do enough for a good firm) Wood, the assistant Chief Draughtsman, and commonly known as Lurch.

"We never had a problem before," grumbled Keith. "Batters would let you get started on a job and when you were half way through it he'd look at it and suggest doing it a different way. So you would have to start again.

"Now Lurch gives the jobs out. He knows how long they should take, and when you started them. But Batters still comes round every day and if you have to start again the job will take longer. If you try and keep to Lurch's deadline, the drawing won't be right, and when the Machine shop complain, John will only say I told you so.

"Another thing, too. If ever we start talking, he tells us to get on with our work. Batters doesn't mind, he'd talk all day about sailing if anybody would listen. What makes it even worse for us is hearing you lot laughing all day. How do you get away with it? Doesn't Grovesy ever tell you off?"

"No. He's as bad as the rest of us. But it doesn't matter. We always get the jobs done on time."

"And another thing, too. You lot can come and go as you please. If we want to go on the shop floor, we have to ask Lurch. He treats us like kids. But I don't think things will go on much longer like this. You just keep an eye out next Friday when we come back from Brian's going away do. You know what Ken Backhouse is like when he's had a couple. He's been threatening to stick one on Lurch for weeks."

"How did he get the name Lurch?"

But before Keith could answer, they were interrupted by Les Fishwick, who had come to tell them who they each had drawn to play in the first round. Keith had drawn John Fox and Alan, Bernard Harrison, a reasonable bowler but one whose level of skill varied in inverse proportion to the amount he had drunk. Soon they were joined by Keith's opponent.

"How are you going to spend the rest of the afternoon after I've hammered you?" But before Keith could reply, he went on: "He's not been boring you with stories about his mate Lurch, has he, Greeno?"

"It's all right for you Foxy, you don't have to put up with him every day like I do."

"Keith, I keep telling you, he'll walk all over you for ever and a day unless you stand up to him. To quote the two great thinkers of the last century, Pluto and Harry Stottle, Lurch is like an old tree. It won't fall down unless you push it."

By this time they had reached the outskirts of Blackpool. The trip itself had followed the same pattern for years. They would start off with lunch at the Green Dragon. This was followed by the bowling competition which would last all afternoon. In the evening they would go into Blackpool and finish up in the Tower Ballroom.

But by the time they had finished their lunch, it had started raining. A few decided to go and watch Blackpool play Sunderland. The rest of them, their brains now affected by the beer, braved the elements. It seemed funny at first, but by the end of the afternoon, they were all wringing wet. As a result the evening was one long miserable experience, particularly when they were refused entry into the Tower. Even the journey back to Ashurst was something to be forgotten.

John Mulholland, like Alan, was on his first trip. He had managed to get into the Tower where he had met an attractive blonde. He had walked her down to her coach and on his way back he had seen Henry, a neighbour of his, in a chip shop. He was as drunk as a lord and hadn't a clue where he was. There was only one thing for it, John decided. Henry would have to come back with them.

As soon as he sat down he began to sing. All the way home his impersonations of Johnny Ray and David Whitefield shattered their ear drums, making it a miserable end to what had been a miserable day. It even finished badly for Henry too, despite John's good neighbour act. Yesterday he and their Alice had just started a week's holiday in Blackpool. Where was she and how the hell had he finished up back in his own bed in Central Street!

On Monday morning, while they were telling Stan and Mick about it, in walked Dave Ainsworth, a sheet metal draughtsman.

"I hope you've got permission to come in here?"

"It's all right, Charlie. Lurch is out for the week. He's gone to Aberthaw power station in South Wales."

"Don't tell me you still haven't sorted him out yet," said Mick. "Surely you've got some brain cells at your end?"

Then Albert Jones from the Wages department, who had come to see Charlie, said, "Don't tell me Lurch is still giving you lads aggravation."

"Tell him what your Linda did to him," said Charlie.

"What was that?" asked Dave.

Albert laughed and then told his tale: "She worked for Lurch when he was in charge of the Standards Lab last year. The Clockwork Man she used to call him. Every

24

day he'd come in, put his apple and Daily Telegraph in his drawer, brush his desk clean, and, if there was the slightest bit of dirt on his blotting pad, he'd change it. Then he'd open all the windows, water his plant and write out his plan for the day in his desk diary. And other than mutter morning he wouldn't say a thing to anybody unless he had to. Then he would read all the test results from the previous day and after that he would go to the toilet and come back just as the tea was coming round. It was the same every day. She used to time him.

"After a bit she decided to get her own back on him. He had been upsetting her for weeks. She started by making a mark on his pad. She did this two or three times in the first week. Then she started to move his apple and then his paper. They could tell he was puzzled, but he didn't let on. After a few days he began to lock his drawer. What he didn't know was that our Linda had a duplicate key.

"The next day she unlocks the drawer, bites the apple and puts it back in the same spot. How they all managed to keep a straight face when he rolled it round and saw these teeth marks in it, I don't know.

"Then she put marker chalk on his phone and he would be walking round all day with a blue ear. Her next trick was to undo the nut on his chair, and when he leaned back he nearly fell off and broke his neck. All the time this was happening he must have thought it was the apprentice they had in there. He would never think it was our Linda. You know what she is like. To look at her, you'd think she couldn't knock a hole in a wet paper bag.

"Then the apprentice joined in. It was his last week in there. He put an old pair of shoes just below the trap door in the toilets, so Lurch thought somebody was in there. Not many ever used that place. It's a bit out of the way. So when the same thing happened every day for a week, he began to get annoyed. He had to walk all the way down to the main toilets and this upset his routine. So on the Friday morning when he sees the same shoes there again, he blows his top.

"'I know you are playing tricks. Come out now, whoever you are,'" he shouts and bangs on the door. Next minute it opens and out comes Frank Rigby, a foremen from the Rolling mill. He had been passing by when a sudden call to nature had overtaken him."

Just as he was finishing, John Mulholland walked in to tell Albert he was wanted on the phone. He then started chatting to Len and Yorky about the girl he'd met in the Tower.

"Where does she come from?" asked Yorky.

"Atherton, but she used to live in Gillarsfield."

"What's her name?" asked Dickie.

"Mavis Case."

"I know her."

"She's married to a wrestler, she's got four kids and used to be a bouncer at the Victoria," laughed Mick.

"And obviously suffers from bad eyesight."

"No, nothing like that, Charlie," said Dickie. "What's unusual is that she has an identical twin."

"I remember when I went out with a twin," chipped in Yorky.

"Another mucky Yorkshire tale coming up, John. I think you're a bit young for this," said Mick.

"I remember the first time I went out with her. Our kid had had a big win on the horses so we'd been drinking all afternoon. By the time I got down town, I were blathered. I'd met her the previous week at a dance and we'd arranged to meet outside Burtons shop in Huddersfield. They had a right big mirror in the window and seeing a person stood outside on the pavement and their reflection in this mirror, it looked as though there were two people there. I didn't know she had a twin sister and just then they were both stood there together.

"When we went past the shop, what with the speed of the bus and this bloody mirror and me seeing double half the time, I thought there were about ten identical women stood there, waiting for me.

"She introduced me to her twin sister and then the pair of us went off for a drink. I didn't take her home but we arranged to meet again on the Monday night and go to the pictures. As we were stood in the queue, she said she had watched That Was The Week That Was on the Saturday night.

"How could you? You were with me in the pub."

"No, she said. That was our Helen you were with!"

6
A HEART ATTACK OCCURS

He was late into work again. It wasn't his fault but then it never was. The bus had stopped for them but the conductor had only allowed four to get on, leaving Alan and a couple of schoolgirls waiting. He could have easily let them all on. He would know that a lot would be getting off at the next stop. But it was the miserable one, so they had no chance.

He never liked going in late. The rest of them would make such a din as he tried to sneak in. But this particular morning it remained quiet as he took the cover off his drawing board.

"Have you heard the news?" said Dickie.

"No. What?"

"The old man has had a heart attack. It sounds serious."

The old man, or Joshua Albert George Wilkinson D.S.O. to give him his full title, had been in charge of the firm for as long as anyone could remember. He had taken over in 1932 on the death of his father. He had been at the helm for so long no-one could imagine life at Wilkinson's without him. But it looked as though they might have to, and the prospects did not look good for he had three sons, none of whom offered much hope for the future.

Firstly, there was Basil. He spent most of his time in London. Wining and dining important people in Government and commerce was what he liked to do. With the object of finding new markets he was forever flying off all over the place. And to achieve success he seemed to visit some of the world's most beautiful and exotic places.

Secondly, there was Cyril, who was forever sticking his nose into things about which he hadn't a clue.

Finally, there was Norman, the Great Pretender. His main interest was in what he called Human Relations and in particular the Staff Association, an area in which it was generally agreed he could do the least damage.

Most of the conversation that morning centred around what might happen. They knew Cyril well. Stan and Mick talked about what he was like when they first moved into the Drawing Office ten years ago.

"There were only a dozen of us here then and we were all in the same office," said

27

Mick. "Cyril would never come and see us. He never understood anything about electrics, but he was forever pestering the mechanical lads. He kept coming up with these hare-brained ideas. He'd get one of them to do all the detail work. They might spend weeks on it, then the next time he'd appear, he had changed his mind or just lost interest. Once you were put on one of his jobs, you'd be wasting your time."

"I don't know,. Ron Dalton never used to think that. He loved working for Cyril," said Stan.

"That was only because he conned him summat rotten."

"Do you remember that time Cyril had the idea of designing a water purifier? Well, actually it was Ronnie that fed him the idea. He let him work on it for weeks, and then had it made in the Machine shop. Unknown to Cyril, Ronnie's sister was married to a water board engineer and they lived on the South Coast, near Brighton. Ronnie gets his brother-in-law to write to Cyril, telling him that he had heard Wilkinson's were designing this interesting piece of equipment and would they like to give it some trials at their water works. Cyril fell for it and let Ronnie take it down there, set it up and monitor its progress. Ronnie stayed at his sister's but he still claimed a load of expenses and came back with a great long technical report that baffled everybody. Shortly after that Cyril went away for a month and when he returned he'd lost all interest. So Ronnie managed a fortnight's holiday, all expenses paid, out of it."

Then they talked about Norman. He was seen by most people as a complete nonentity, a person who would be indistinguishable in a crowd of three.

"He wasn't always such a drip," said Mick, "Not when he had the religious bug."

"Do you remember that time he tried to convert your mate Ludwig?" said Stan.

"Ludwig. Who the heck was that?" asked Dickie.

"It was Les Earnshaw, one of the sheet metal draughtsmen."

"How did he get that name?"

"It was from the time Norman was on one of his crusades. He used to come into the drawing office a couple of times a week and buttonhole somebody. Of course, we would all agree with what he said just to get shut of him, but not Les. He was always one for arguing. One day he told Norman that in his view Man had created God in his own image. Norman thought for a moment and then said that surely it was the other way round, that God had created Man in his own image. But Les didn't agree.

"Now Norman's way of arguing was to quote from the Bible. If it was in there it must be right. So Les digs one of his books out and says to Norman, 'Let me just quote you this. You are always quoting from your book. Now it's my turn.'"

At this point Mick produced a tattered pamphlet from his drawer. "This is the book he used. He gave it to me when he left. I've been intending to read it for years, but never got round to it. So Les reads this passage out: 'Nothing exists outside

Nature and Man, and the higher beings created by our religious fantasies are only the fantastic reflections of our own essence.' That baffled Norman and everybody else as well."

"Give Norman his due though, Mick. He tried. He kept coming back, but he wasn't in the same league as Les."

"It went on for weeks," continued Mick. "It would start every lunchtime. Sometimes him and Les would be at it all afternoon. You could never get anything done for listening to them. And Les used to spend all morning preparing for it. But then he went and spoiled it all."

"How come?" asked Alan.

"At the end of the month you had to fill out a time sheet and Les had hardly drawn a thing. So he asked Norman if he could give him a little help. 'Certainly', said Norman, 'that's what Christianity is all about, helping people.' 'Well, I'm having a little difficulty filling out my time sheet. Do you think you could give me a job number for all this time we have spent talking.' After that Norman stopped coming."

"And how did he get the nickname Ludwig?"

"It was from the title of his book, 'Ludwig Feurbach and the End of German Classical Philosophy'. He said it was written by his Uncle Fred."

"Who?"

"It was a guy called Fredrich Engels."

"Who's he, when he's at home?"

"Some big buddy of Karl Marx according to Les."

"A bit heavy going for a draffie, wasn't it?"

"Not for Les. He was very well read. In fact, he started writing a book just before he left. I don't know if he ever finished it but he had great plans for it."

"What was it called?"

"One Hundred and One Ways of Avoiding Work," laughed Stan.

There were no funny stories to tell about Basil. He was not someone to cross or have a joke with. When dealing with people he acted like a graduate member of the Kalashnikov school of human relations. Thankfully he rarely ventured North.

Len knew what would happen next: "Basil will come up here and take control until it's clear how ill the old man is. He won't let the other two get their hands on anything important or make any decisions. He knows if they do, we'll all be down the road by Christmas. No, he'll get some plan organised with his Dad and then he'll bring one of his posh friends in to supervise it all. Then he'll buzz off back to his big house and his fancy women. I'll lay money on it."

And that day Basil did appear, having spent the night at the family home at Daresbury in Cheshire. Within an hour of arriving he had spoken to John Walker, the

Personnel Manager, Charlie Pickles, the Engineering Manager, George Kilpatrick, the Shipping Manager, and Harold Rimmer, who was in charge of Research and Development. This was followed by a meeting of all the senior managers, where he told them that Charlie Pickles would be in overall charge until the end of the year, by which time the extent of the old man's illness would be known. Basil himself would be returning to London at the end of the week. There was a possibility of a large order for the South African railways to be won and he had some important people to see. Then he announced that money was to be made available for modernising the Foundry and the Laboratory, and since Harold Rimmer was retiring at the end of January, with immediate effect he would be aided by his ultimate successor, Arthur Wood!

The news broke out around the time everybody was getting ready to leave. Alan found himself sat next to Keith on the bus going home. He had a great smile on his face. "Heard the news, Greeno. Lurch has got Rimmer's job. At last we're shut of the bastard. And another thing, it looks as though we are going to start going out on site as well. I'm off to Bold on Thursday."

"I hope you won't get travel sick going there?"

"I'm getting used to travelling. You'll never guess where I went last Saturday?"

"No. Where?"

"Blackpool."

"Blackpool! I thought you'd have seen enough of that place for a bit. Who did you go with?"

"I went with my mother and our Jimmy. You'll never guess what she has started doing again, watching the Saints."

"What, at her age. How old is she now?"

"Sixty seven next month."

"And what's brought this on?"

"Well it's all a bit strange really. We were both up at her place a couple of weeks ago and she says, 'I've made a will and everything will be equally shared between the three of you. Don't start worrying, I'm not ill. I just want everything in order, so you all know where you stand', and then she said 'There's one thing I'd like to do before I go, I'd like to watch the rugby again.'

"To tell you the truth I thought she was going doolally. All this had come right out of the blue, but what can you do? So we took her up to Blackpool on Saturday in the car. She really enjoyed herself, couldn't take her eyes off Vollenhoven. When we got back to her place she gives our Jimmy a pound and says, 'Are we all right for Tuesday? I've not been to Watersheddings since before the War. I wonder if it's changed'. Her and my Dad used to go watching the Saints all over when they were courting. So that's where we are going tomorrow night."

30

"Does she she stand on the terraces, or do you have to go in the stand with her?"

But before Keith could reply they were interrupted by the arrival of the conductress. Alan could tell straight away that Keith knew her when he asked for half fare and could she ask the driver to go a bit faster since his mum didn't like him to be out late after school. As she carried on down the bus Alan asked about her.

"Helen Murdoch. I went out with her last year for a couple of months. She's a bit of hot stuff. Do you fancy her? I'll get you fixed up with her if you like. She's not going out with anybody, which is unusual for her."

But before Alan could respond the bus was approaching his stop. He dashed down the stairs and jumped off just as it was pulling away. He looked back as it moved down Mill Lane. Helen had followed him down the stairs and was now stood on the platform. He had often seen her on the bus before and he quite liked the look of her. Did she wave, or was it just wishful thinking? He wondered if Keith meant it. He was always trying to get his ex-girl friends fixed up.

The following day more details began to emerge. John Battersby called a meeting to tell the mechanical section how things would change now that they would no longer have the delicate hand of Mr Wood to help them. He finished, with a smile on his face, by saying that if anyone wanted to organise a going away do or a collection he would have no objection and he would be quite happy to be the last to contribute.

A little while later, Keith walked down to his board and said, "It's make your mind up time tonight Greeno. I told Helen you want to go out with her and what a generous person you are with your money. Do you know what she said? 'He's only got to ask, and all will be revealed'. You can take that whatever way you want. She always did have a way with words. She should be on the stage, not a bus platform. But you'll have to ask her tonight. She's switching to the Atherton route tomorrow."

The rest of his day went by as quick as a flash. He couldn't get her out of his mind, especially after Keith told him what she had done at his twenty first party. Before he knew it, he was walking out of the Aspinall Street gates. He groaned when he saw there were two buses waiting. Fortunately he could see Helen stood on the platform of the second one. He hung back a bit until the first one had filled up and as he got on she smiled and said, "Hello, where's Errol Flynn to-night?" He mumbled something about Keith being kept in for talking and then went upstairs.

After a few minutes she came on to the top deck and worked her way down to the front where he was sat on his own. He gave her a shilling for his fare. She sat down on the seat alongside him as she counted out his change and slowly turned the handle of her ticket machine. His heart was beating like mad and he knew it was now or never. He had kept mouthing what he wanted to say to her all afternoon. And while he was plucking up the courage, he watched her sexily swinging her leg to and fro.

31

"Keith said this is your last night on this route."

"Yes. I'll be going past Tyldseley Bonks this time tomorrow. So you'll not see me up here for a bit."

It really was now or never.

"Well, I might do. How do you fancy coming out with me sometime."

She smiled but shrugged her shoulders. Did that mean no? It didn't. It meant the very opposite.

He watched her tongue brushing over her lips, and after what seemed an age, she smiled, nodded and said, "All right. When?"

"What are you doing on Saturday night?"

"Nothing special."

"How about meeting at seven o clock, outside the Gas Showrooms."

She stood up and said, "OK." Then she put her hand on his shoulder, leaned forward closely to his face and said, "That's unless the bus is late".

Three minutes later, as he stood on the platform waiting for the bus to slow down, she nudged his shoulder and said, "and don't forget to have plenty of change in your pocket."

7
KEIGHLEY REVISITED

As he walked into the office the next day Mick was there waiting for him.

"Don't take your coat off, we're not stopping."

"Why, where are we going?"

"That foundry in Keighley. I hope you've got your passport with you."

Five minutes later Norman Stone, one of Wilkinson's sales engineers, was explaining the purpose of their visit, Mick's second visit as it turned out.

"They can't make their mind up how they want us to do the job. I want you two to look at that control room again and find a better place to install our control gear. When you've finished we'll discuss it after lunch with their M.D."

They spent the morning with the Foundry Manager, who kept getting dragged away to deal with other matters. Standing around can be very tiring in a dirty, fume laden, draughty atmosphere. By half twelve they were both in great need of sustenance. Last time Mick had come he had eaten in the works' canteen, but this time they went down to the pub with the chargehand, Les.

As he put two pints before them he said, "I bet you've got nowt as good as this in Lancashire?"

Mick picked up his glass and in two gulps had drunk it.

"By gum, I needed that. I was spitting feathers. And it's not a bad pint either. I wish I'd come here before".

Before Alan could make any comment, the foreman was ordering another round.

"The firm's paying for these and your dinner as well so don't be shy."

"And there was me thinking all Yorkshire folk had short arms and long pockets" laughed Mick.

By the time their meal was ready they were drinking their third pint. It was Timothy Taylor's bitter, tasty and, as they were later to discover, strong as well.

"I've been in this pub before," said Mick as he came back from the toilets. "We came here after a match".

"Who do you follow?"

"Wigan."

"Not a bad team, nearly as good as mine."

"Who's that?"

"Bramley!" He laughed and then turned to Alan and asked him if he was a rugby fan as well.

"Yes, when I'm not playing football."

"Do you follow Wigan?"

"No. St. Helens."

"I don't suppose it's any use asking either of you two who is the better winger, Boston or Vollenhoven."

"Not really," said Mick, "but to be fair they are both good, though I think Boston has just got the edge."

"I've seen Boston play a couple of times. I've not seen Vollenhoven yet."

"Well you've got a treat in store."

"Have you always followed Bramley, Les?"

"Yes. I'm a true Villager. I used to live opposite Barley Mow when I were a kid."

He then went on to tell them about his brief spell as a player, a few games at the end of 1938 - 39 season in the 'A' team when he was nineteen and the highlight of his career, scoring four tries at York. "I might have made it, but a German bullet put an end to all that for me."

Soon it was time to go back to work. They took their leave of Les; he'd been good company, particularly after they had discovered their common interest in the greatest game. They went up to the meeting room and sat there while the financial details of the amended order were thrashed out in great detail. By the time it was concluded the two of them could be heard gently snoring.

The moment he walked into the office the following morning Dickie said, "I hear you and Mick are sleeping together."

Alan laughed. "I couldn't keep my eyes open. After three pints and listening to Norman's droning voice I just dozed off."

"Whose beer was it?" asked Yorky.

"Timothy Taylor's, they brew it in Keighley."

"Lunatic soup we used to call it. It is good. Too strong for you Lancashire lads by the sound of it. I used to drink it when we lived in Mytholmroyd."

"I bet you can't spell that," said Mick, but before Yorky showed that he could, in walked Tommy Wiseman with a bundle of drawings. Alan had spent his last year as an apprentice with Tommy when he was still an electrician. Now he was in charge of the commissioning of the switchgear in the copper refinery. As a result he was a frequent visitor to the D.O. During the course of the next hour he would point out any mistakes in their drawings and tell them of any changes that had been made.

"Are the apprentices still giving you a hard time?" asked Alan, sometime later as Joan was pouring out the tea.

"No apprentice has ever got one over on me. You ought to know that. Don't forget I am the wise man, and you are still green. I'll show my backside in Burton's window the day any apprentice tricks me. I tell you what though, none of this new lot will. Have you come across any of them yet?"

None of them had, although they had heard about them. In September, Wilkinson's had taken on six university graduates. They were all very upper class or liked to act as though they were and soon came to be known as the chaps.

"There's one of them in the Machine Shop," said Len. "Billy Fryer told me he put him with Cedric on his first day. After lunch the bugger went back to Billy and told him that he now knew everything there was to learn about sharpening drills, could he go on a lathe."

"The one we've got with us had only been here a week when he told Ronnie Garner the layout of that big display panel in the operator's cabin was wrong," said Tommy. "That didn't go down too well with Ronnie. He'd designed it."

Harry Groves went into his office and came back holding a piece of paper. "We've got one of them coming in here in February, Miles Phillipson."

"Miles, what sort of bloody name is that?" said Dickie.

"That's typical. The one we've got is called James, but he doesn't like being called Jimmy," said Tommy. "You know they come from a totally different world to us lot. It's unbelievable. Their daddies don't work in a factory, they usually own it. They all went to public school and some of them are so bloody arrogant with it as well. Toffee-nosed twits."

"I went to public school," said Tony. "Newton Road Juniors."

Ignoring him, Tommy continued, "You know our Paul is an apprentice with the Coal Board now. When he'd been there a month, him and all the other first year lads were sent on a General Engineering course to St. Helens Tech. In his class were some of these comedians. On the first day they had little Charlie Ainsworth. He's been there for years. He's a great bloke. There's nothing he doesn't know about lathes and milling machines.

"Now Charlie can only reach half way up the blackboard so he soon fills it. He wipes off what he had written after they have all had time to copy it and then carries on. Just in front of the board is this bookcase. The next thing, one of these snooty bastards sticks his hand up. 'Excuse me sir, why don't you stand on the bookcase and then you could reach the top of the board?' Charlie just says, 'Nay lad, you can't do that. You can't stand on that book case'.

"In the afternoon, they had Harry Byrom. He's a right scruffy bugger, but just like Charlie, he knows what he is talking about, though I bet half of them thought he had come to empty the bin when he walked in. He starts off straight-away writing on the board. Within five minutes the bottom half was full, so he stands on that bookcase and carries on. This snooty bugger, sticks his hand up again. Harry turns round, sees him and says, 'Aye, lad what is it?' 'This morning, Mr Ainsworth said that you cannot stand on that bookcase.' 'Well,' replied Harry, with his thumb in each of his braces, twanging them as he spoke, 'Thee tell him tha's seen it can be done.'"

As everybody laughed the phone rang. "It's the apprentice for you Tommy," shouted Tony, "Can you go back to your place, and can you call in the canteen and collect his tea and crumpets? And can you go straight away as he is feeling peckish?"

"It'll be Frank. I said I would be back before ten. We're testing the alarms." And with that he left.

"So where are you taking this bus conductress?" asked Charlie. "Will it be the ballet or the opera?"

"How do you know about her?"

Charlie smiled and tapped the side of his nose with his little finger.

"It was revealed to me yesterday while you were out of the country."

"I bet it was Keith."

"It wasn't actually, but it doesn't really matter. You wouldn't have kept that quiet all day."

"Who said I was going to?"

"Now listen carefully, I'm only going to say this once. Our Derek is having his twenty first do on Saturday and you are invited. Tony, Dickie and their Sarah and a few of the mechanical lads are coming. Your old mate Roy Penketh and his wife will be there as well so you'll be in good company. Why don't you bring her?"

"Where's it at?"

"The Conservative Club in Dob Lane."

"I can't take somebody there on our first date. What sort of a fool will she think I am. I've got some principles."

"I knew you'd say that. Look it's only a booze up and you are better bringing her to something like this where there's plenty folk around and you can see how she performs in public."

"Aye, and then when you take her home, you can find out how she performs in private," joked Yorky.

"From what I've heard about her, quite well and quite often," laughed Dickie.

"I'll think about it," said Alan. He knew it would be a good do, but he wasn't sure if he wanted to take Helen there, not on their first date.

Shortly after, Keith walked over to his board.

"I thought you were going to Bold today?"

"No, it's been put off until next week. They couldn't find the red carpet."

36

"What an exciting life the mechanical section are now leading," said Len.

"I'll tell you what, I was excited at Oldham on Tuesday night. What a cracking game. And by the way Mick, in case you didn't know, the Saints won, yet again."

"Did your Mam enjoy it?"

"She did an' all. I've never heard her shout so much. She even called Charlie Winslade a little bastard. We were stood right near him and he heard her."

"What did he do?"

"He just laughed. So it's Swinton at Central Park on the twenty seventh. What with Lurch going and the Saints back in form, things are looking good. And they are looking good for you, Greeno aren't they. I bet you can't wait for Saturday night when all will be revealed. Where are you taking her?"

"I suppose we'll go to the flix."

"Do you want a bit of advice from an old Don Juan, Greeno. On your first date, treat her as though she was really special. If you do go to the pictures splash out, take her upstairs in the two and nines. When the film is over, talk to her about the philosophical content of the film, its political message and social significance for humanity. And most important, when you get off the bus at the other end, go and buy her a bag of chips. That will really show her how much you think of her."

"So that was your secret was it, Charlie. That's how you charmed your women. I often wondered. I knew it wasn't your good looks."

"You are wrong with this one Charlie," went on Keith. "She'll not do it for a bag of chips. He'll have to buy her a fish and some mushy peas as well. It's going to be a dear night for the poor lad."

Friday was a much better day. It was Brian Cunliffe's going away do, so he bought them all a pint. Then Charlie reminded them all it was Len's birthday, so he had to do the honours for the rest of the section. As they were stood at the bar, Yorky remarked, "Two free pints and Poet's day as well."

"What the heck is Poet's day?" asked Dickie.

"Piss Off Early, Tomorrow's Saturday."

"Saturday," thought Alan, "my night out with Helen. I wonder what she's really like?" If half of what Keith had said was true, he was in for a good time. But then Keith said the same thing about all the women he had been out with. He couldn't wait to find out for himself.

But as things turned out he never did do.

8
A BLESSING IN DISGUISE

Alan was woken on Saturday morning by the sound of rain on the window. He opened the curtains, took one look at the weather and fell back onto his bed. He closed his eyes again and thought about the day in front of him. There were two things to look forward to, the match in the afternoon and his date in the evening.

He had played football for as long as he could remember. In September he had signed on with a new club, Astley United. They had won their first five matches on the trot and today were up against Park Rangers, who were also unbeaten but had dropped a point in their last game against Havanna Miners Welfare Reserves.

Park Rangers played in Ramsdale Park but they changed in a large wooden hut about a quarter of a mile away. When they arrived at the pitch to say that it was water-logged it was the understatement of the year. It was obvious they could not play. The referee took one look at it, told them he couldn't swim and called it off. But when they arrived back at the hut it was locked. One of the home team went to get the key from the caretaker, only to be told by the man's daughter that her dad had gone into town but would be back before they had finished.

There was no way of getting into the place. All they could do was go back and attempt to play football. It was ridiculous, but there was no other way to pass the time. Then half way through the game, with United defending the deep end, Alan went over on his ankle and before long he was in an ambulance heading for Victoria Hospital.

An hour later he was lying on a bed with his left leg strapped up and a nurse telling him that he would be all right and that he hadn't broken anything.

"It hurts like hell."

"Well it will do. You have torn your ligaments but you'll survive. You can go now but you must rest for a few days, and no jitterbugging to-night either!"

"How can I get home? I've no bus fare."

"You won't need to. There's somebody waiting for you outside."

She gave him a pair of crutches and helped him into the waiting room where he saw his Uncle Norman reading the Football Pink.

"You can stay in here," said his mum as she directed him into the front room. "Otherwise I'll spend half the day traipsing up and down the stairs and it'll be easier if anybody comes to see you."

Shortly afterwards the team's goalkeeper, Eric Barrow, turned up with his clothes. He had one piece of good news for Alan. Sacred Heart, who until today were also unbeaten, had lost to Gas and Electric, so with a game in hand Astley United were still top of Division Three.

His next visitor appeared in the morning. It was Phil Whalley, the centre forward, with his shoes. "I don't know how they finished up in my bag," he explained.They talked for a while and then Alan said, "It looks as though you're going to have to do without me for a bit. I don't think I'll be even fit to come and watch."

"They'll have to do without me as well, I won't be here."

"Why, where are you going?"

"Australia."

"Australia! When did you decide that?"

"Last night after the girlfriend told me she was in the club."

"You always said that would never happen to you."

"Well it has done, and it's just about now that the shit will be hitting the fan. She's going to tell her mother when she comes back from church."

He left shortly afterwards, a young man whose whole life style was suddenly to be totally changed. And on Saturday December 8th, Astley United did have to play without the pair of them. Phil had a good reason to account for why he couldn't wear the number nine shirt that day. He was one of the two main participants in a religous ceremony in St.Lukes Parish Church.

Shortly after his sister Joan called round with the baby and while she was there Auntie Doris appeared. He struggled into the living room for his tea after they had gone and was just settling down to watch the television for the evening when in walked his mates Geoff, Ken and Ronnie armed with a crate of brown ale.

"So what are you going to do with all your spare time?" asked Ronnie as he dealt the cards. "That is when you have not got Listen With Mother and Mrs. Dales Diary on."

"I'm going to do our family tree. It's something I've fancied doing for ages."

"Why?"

"It's interesting, that's why?"

"It wouldn't interest me."

"The only reason you wouldn't want to do yours is because you'd probably find half of your relatives were still in London Zoo."

Alan had always been interested in knowing about his family and this would be an ideal time to do some research. And asking all his relatives questions about themselves would prevent them telling him about all the accidents, illnesses and operations that

39

they had had or heard about over the years. He started work on it on Monday. He hadn't been at it long, when his next visitor turned up. But it wasn't a relative, it was Ken's Dad. After asking him how he felt, Arthur said: "I thought you would like to be the first to hear the news. They've decided to keep the station and the branch line open."

"That's great, when did you hear that?"

"This morning. I had a good idea they wouldn't go through with it. They were suprised at the amount of opposition."

"It was your petition that did it," smiled his mum.

"Well, you might be right, Mrs. Greenall. Do you know we finally collected over twenty thousand signatures?"

Then he rummaged about in his bag and handed a book to Alan.

"What's this?"

"The Ragged Trousered Philantrophists."

"That's a funny title," said his mum. "What's it about?"

"It's about how the rich live in luxury at our expense. It's a bit out of date now, but it's still good. It was written by a Liverpool bloke, Robert Tressell, and he was only a painter and decorator."

He read it the following day. It was a fascinating book. He could understand why Ken's dad had described it as a classic. The description of the foreman, Nimrod, who sneaked round trying to catch the men whistling, made him smile. That must be who Lurch modelled himself on.

Over the next few days, Alan began to piece together all the information his relatives had told him. Some of it he already knew about, others came as a complete suprise. What really pleased him was their response. Some came back two or three times, often returning with old certificates recording births, marriages and deaths. Cuttings from old papers began to appear, photographs, even a couple of medals from some long forgotten war. His asking the questions jogged their memories. Slowly they began to recall things from the dim and distant past, special occasions, deeds of heroism, what they did in the General Strike and how they managed during the Depression. And he also heard about the tragedy that had taken the life of little Sophie nearly a hundred years ago.

Auntie Hilda called round most days. She kept saying that she couldn't remember but she could. Really she was quite amazing with what she knew. From her, he learned an enormous amount about her and Granny's parents and grandparents. And the gaps in her memory could often be filled by asking Auntie Doris.

From his questions, he was pleased to have it confirmed that he came from good proletarian stock. He knew both his Grandad and his great grandfather, old Tom, had

40

worked for years at the old Beswick colliery. And before that, old Tom's father too had worked underground until a rock fall meant he was never able to work or walk again.

On his Granny's side, he knew that her father had been a bricklayer, but labourer would perhaps be the best way to describe how the rest of her side of the family earned their daily crust.

Around tea time Charlie called in on his way home from work. "I heard what had happened to you in the club on Sunday night." Typical Charlie then went on to describe what a great do Alan had missed and how much they had all drunk.

"But look on the bright side. You would have had a terrible hangover on Sunday morning."

On Wednesday Keith appeared. "You haven't seen Helen, have you?" was Alan's first question.

"I've not seen her, but Phil Quinn has. She was in town on Sunday night with a lad from Sutton."

Within a few days the swelling began to go down and after a couple of weeks he was ready to go back to work. He had enjoyed the break from work, and he had enjoyed constructing the family tree. He had been able to trace his relatives back to 1791 when his great great great grandfather Albert Silas Holding had been born at Collins Green. On Granny's side he found out that his great great great grandmother had come from Wales around the same time, but why nobody knew. He found it all very interesting but he was missing all the fun and games at work.

Unfortunately his return was a rather muted affair since only half of the section were in. Yorky was at a funeral in Wakefield, Stan had taken the week off to look after his wife who had fallen ill again and Mick was on jury service. On top of that Charlie had toothache, went to the dentists and didn't come back for two days. But by Friday it was nearly back to normal except that Stan was still off. But then the D.O. was graced by the visit of Basil Wilkinson. He spent an hour going round the mechanical section and promised to return after lunch to see what the electrical side were doing. They decided it might be better if they weren't all smelling of beer when he appeared so they went without their Friday session. But he never came back and so for Alan the whole week had been one big anti-climax.

"I wish I'd stayed off another week," he said to Keith as they stood in the bus queue.

"Well, now you know how we used to feel when Lurch was in charge."

"How are things up at your end now?"

"Great. I'm almost enjoying coming here."

"Did you go to Bold ?"

"Yes. I was there yesterday, third time in a month. And I'm going to Thorpe

Marsh power station in Yorkshire next week with Brian Cunliffe."

"I thought Brian had left."

"Well, you know Brian. He's always got some devious plot on the go. We all thought he'd left to get away from Lurch, but that was only half of it. He's just bought a house and wanted some ready cash. So he left in order to get his pension money out. As soon as he heard about Lurch, he rang up and asked John for his job back."

The bus finally arrived and they went upstairs.

"Have you heard any more about Helen while I've been off?"

"You've missed your chance there, Greeno. She's going out with a lad from Sutton. He's a fitter at Pilks and he's got a car. Our Judith saw them in the Punch Bowl last week, all lovey dovey she said they were."

As they were talking, the conductress came up for their fares.

"Hello Betty," Keith said. "How long have you been on the buses. I thought you were still working on the pit brow."

"About eight weeks. What about you? Are you still at school?"

As she was working her way down the bus Alan looked at her legs and said, "Very nice."

"I know what you're thinking Greeno but don't bother to ask. She's been going out with a lad from Nook End for the last six months. And unlike you, he's got good looks, charm and intelligence."

Alan changed the subject to the big event of the weekend, the Lancashire County Cup Final between St. Helens and Swinton.

"Is your mam going?"

"You might as well ask if it's going to get light in the morning."

"Do you fancy their chances?"

"I do, but it'll be a close game. They'll have to keep their eye on Albert Blan. If him and Ken Gowers are on form, Swinton could just do it."

They chatted on for a bit and then Keith said, "What time are you going? You'd better get there early. There'll be a big crowd. There could be thirty thousand there if it's a nice day."

"We're meeting in the Crawford at twelve, so we'll be in good time."

"You will if you don't start drinking."

Then he smiled and said, "I went next door last night. Their little lad, he's nearly eight. He's not been watching the Saints long, but he's really keen. He told me he's going to get there for one o clock. He wants to watch them raise the curtain!"

9
WATCHING THE SAINTS AGAIN

Even before he opened his eyes, he knew what the weather was doing. He could hear the rain lashing against the window and the tree in next door's garden blowing in the wind. By the time he left the house three hours later, the rain had eased but it was still blustery and the sky was black and threatening.

As they came out of the station they joined an enormous army of Swinton fans walking up Wallgate. All the way through Wigan town centre the wearers of the red and white and the blue and white mingled together. There was always a good atmosphere before these big matches, although today the weather was putting a bit of a dampener on it.

They stood under the big stand on the Popular side. There were hundreds of Saints fans all around them, many of whom Alan knew or recognised. After a few minutes a man dressed as though it was the middle of summer shouted up to Roy as he walked by.

"Who's that?" asked Ken. "He must be frozen."

"It's Move Up."

"Who?"

"Move Up. Have you not heard him? Whenever we are defending, at a play the ball, you'll hear him shouting 'Move Up, Move Up Saints, Move Up'," and with his hand Roy indicated what the St.Helens players had to do.

"I've heard him," remembered Geoff. "He's like a bloody gramophone record."

"He was like that when they all lived in that pokey little house in Clyde street. He had to sleep with his little brother. When he came to bed there was never any room, so he always had to wake the lad up and say 'Move Up, Move Up.'"

Before any of them could ask Roy how he knew that all conversations on the terraces came to an end as the voice on the loudspeaker boomed out:

"Good afternoon and welcome to Central Park. Today's teams line up as follows: St.Helens - Coslett, Van Vollenhoven, Donovan, Smith, Sullivan, Benyon, Heaton, Arkwright, Dagnall, Watson, Tembey, Huddart and Major. Swinton - Gowers, McMahon, Halliwell, Buckley, Speed, Parkinson, Cartwright, K.Roberts, T.Roberts,

Morgan, Norburn, Bonser and Blan. And the referee is Mr.Matt Coates from Pudsey."

Suddenly there was a great roar as the Swinton team came out of the tunnel, quickly followed by the men from Knowsley Road. The conditions by now were atrocious. There was little to choose between the two teams, and there were few scoring chances. This was not due to any lack of effort or skill. It was just the combination of the wind, the rain and the mud that made playing good open Rugby League impossible. In the end it was one bit of magic by Vollenhoven, latching onto a wild pass by the Swinton prop Ken Roberts, that proved to be the difference. And so for the third year on the trot, St.Helens beat Swinton to win the Lancashire Cup, this time by seven points to four.

"So where are we off to-night?" asked Geoff after they had watched the Saints captain, Bill Major, lift the trophy.

"Let's go to the Emp."

"I knew you'd say that, Greeno. You'd live there if they took lodgers in."

"Why not? It's a great place."

"Tell us about Bill Unsworth's band again, Greeno. Tell us how it's better than Johnny Dankworth's," laughed Roy.

"Never mind that," said Geof,f "let's go and get some grub. I'm starving, and none of that Chinese rubbish for me, Greeno. I'm going to that pie shop on the Market."

After they had eaten, they went into the Bodega, supped five pints of Magee Marshalls bitter and by half past eight were in Lancashire's premier dance hall. They had never been in there so early and most of those stood around them were women. The next dance was a ladies' choice, and to their suprise an attractive blonde asked Alan to dance. It was the last they saw of him.

Sunday evening found Alan, Roy, Ronnie and Geoff in the Raven. They usually met there, swapped highly exaggerated stories about their previous night's exploits and began to make plans for the coming week's entertainment.

"How did you make out last night, Greeno?" asked Geoff. "I saw you sloping off early. She looked a bit classy for you. Are you seeing her again?"

"I might do. Trouble is, she lives near Preston."

"You didn't take her home, did you?"

"Not quite. She's staying at her sisters at Coppull for a couple of weeks."

"How did you get back?"

"On the bus."

"What, at that time! The last bus from Chorley is at eleven. I used to catch it when I was going out with that nurse Pauline."

"It wasn't a Corporation bus. I don't know where it came from. It was a bit of a mystery."

"What do you mean?"

"Well, for a start there was no conductor on it. None of the passengers were English. I tried talking to a couple of them, but they couldn't understand a word of what I was saying."

"Who does."

"And they all stared at me from the moment I got on, as though I was an alien from another planet."

"That sounds reasonable."

"And not one of them spoke all the time I was on it."

"They were probably Swinton fans."

"There were no markings, inside or outside, it had no registration plates and there was a really wierd smell everywhere."

"It must have been the start of The Invasion of the Body Snatchers. You don't half tell us some cock and bull stories. How many had you had last night?"

Ignoring Ronnie's comment, Alan asked what had happened to Ken.

"He went off with that ginger-haired beauty from UpHolland, you know, that one that lives on a farm."

"What about you?"

"I met a teacher from Ashton. I'm sure she's going to teach me a few things. The first lesson's on Thursday night."

The conversation moved on to the week ahead. They decided they would go to watch the Saints play Leeds at Headingley. Now it was just going to be like the old days again when going to the match became the main event of the week. After Leeds, it was Warrington at home, a dour encounter with the Wires winning by four points to two. Then another trip into Yorkshire, Wheldon Road in Castleford, with the Saints squeezing home by eight seven thanks to two tries by Len Killeen and a goal by Kel Coslett.

The following Saturday the Saints were at home to Huddersfield. Alan was stood in the bus queue behind the Sephton Arms along with Ken, Roy, Geoff and his brother Pete when someone tapped him on the shoulder.

"Hello, Greeno, long time, no see."

It was Neil Morris, who had been in their class at Lane Head. They hadn't seen each other for years, but Mogger, as he had always been known, still had that silly grin on his face.

"Hello, Neil. How are you doing? I thought you'd emigrated?"

"No. We went living in Haresfinch when I was twelve. My mam got married again and me and her moved in with his family."

"And what are you doing for a living?"

"I'm a turner at the B.I. What about you?"

"I'm a draughtsman at Wilkinson's."

"Oh, an office job, very nice."

"I see you've given up wearing clogs."

"Aye, there's been a few changes since I was at Lane Head."

"And have you learned to read yet?"

"You bugger."

They both laughed. Mogger had been the worst reader in the whole school. He was hopeless. The rest of the classs would all watch as he slowly moved his finger along the pages, mouthing each letter until the sound in his head coincided with a word he knew. Alan remembered one time listening to him reading a description of the River Nile and when he came to the name of the country he had called it egg white. But to show how things had changed, he took a piece of paper from his pocket and proceeded to read the details of how and where to pay his gas bill.

"How long have you been watching the Saints?"

"Not long. I was playing until the end of last season with Rochdale."

"Were you in the first team?"

"I had a couple of games for them and then I went and broke my shoulder at Hunslet."

He raised his left arm awkwardly. "Can you hear it clicking? It won't go any higher than that. It gives me gip some days, specially when it's damp. It's a good job it's no worse. I can't afford to be off work, I'm getting wed soon."

"Who's the lucky lady?"

"Eh, She might be one of your relatives. Clare Greenall. She lives at the back of St.Helens Town football ground."

"I don't think she is. There are Greenalls all over Lancashire."

"Well there'll be one less in April."

As they walked on to the terraces, Alan saw Ronnie talking to his uncle, who usually came with him to the home games. He told Neil to hold back for a minute.

"Harpo, guess who I've seen in town this morning?"

"Who?"

"Your old mate Mogger."

While they had been at the junior school Ronnie and Neil had alternated between being best mates and worst enemies. Ronnie's most lasting memory of Mogger stemmed from an incident just after they had left Lane Head. Due to Mogger's trickery, Ronnie had finished up in Taylor's building yard covered in wet cement.

"What did you always say you'd do to him if ever you saw him again?" And as he

46

said that he nodded to where Mogger was stood.

"I said I would knock hell out of him, but I think I've just changed my mind."

"Hello, Harpo. My, haven't you grown into a big boy."

"You haven't been hiding from me all these years have you?"

They shook hands and soon the three of them began to reminisce about their school days. Since Neil had been living away from Ashurst he was very interested to hear what had happened to his former school mates.

"John Ashcroft is in the Merchant Navy, Steve Roscoe and Jimmy Mellor are both at Bank Top, Noel Kenny is an electrician at Mathers and Ray Forshaw works in the offices at our place," said Alan.

"Barry Winstanley went back to Durham with his mother after his dad was killed at Clock Face. Ray Ellison drives a van for the Gas Board, Billy Davenport is a fitter at Vicars and the clever one, John Middlehurst, went to University and he's living down South now."

"Do you remember that time we played cricket against Newton Road school one Saturday morning and he turned up in a car in a white shirt, white flannels, white boots and his own bat."

"I do," said Ronnie, "and he got bowled out first ball."

"He always thought he was a cut above the rest of us," said Mogger. "Stuck up get."

"Well, he did always come top of the class," said Alan.

"Do you ever see any of the girls - Joan Mills, Marjorie Barton or little Janice."

"Joan still lives behind the school. She works at Hiltons. Marjorie has got a couple of kids. She married a GI from Burtonwood. And Janice's family emigrated to Australia last year," said Ronnie.

"Norma Tickle works in her dad's shop, Lynn Atherton is a tracer at Mathers and Dorothy Harris is still living in that little house in Dob Lane," said Alan. "She works at Pilkingtons. I think she's at Ravenhead."

At this Neil put his thumb and finger to his nose and as they all laughed he said: "I wonder if she's still got them purple patches on her head?"

"Didn't you meet Sally Bickershaw when you were going round with your petition?" asked Ronnie.

Before Alan could reply, Neil said, "I heard about you and that petition. One of the shop stewards brought it in to work and we all signed it. Big working class hero eh Greeno. I hope the fame didn't go to your head."

"I'll tell you who else I saw going round, Norman Talbot. You wouldn't believe how much he's changed. He's gone all religious. He wouldn't even sign the petition, said it was political and he couldn't take sides on any earthly matters."

Then Mogger told them that Alan Martin had died. He had been with them right from the early days at Lane Head. When they were in Miss Bolton's class he began to be off sick a lot. Each time he came back he was thinner and paler. He managed to attend the first three weeks in Mrs. Walton's class and then he stopped coming altogether. After that they often saw him being pushed round in an old fashioned wheelchair by a shabbily dressed couple who could have been either his parents or his grandparents.

"What was wrong with him? I often used to wonder about him, and those two people who used to push him round," asked Alan.

"He had polio. My auntie told me. He was on her ward for ages. That couple were his parents, his mother must have been over forty when she had him."

They talked on until their conversation was halted by the loudspeaker welcoming the visitors from Fartown and giving out the changes to the programme.

Having Mogger with them added a new dimension to their afternoon's entertainment. The others had only played the game at school or in the park. Mogger had mixed it with some of the best. He watched the game with a keener eye, and he picked out things that were happening much quicker. By the end of the match, Alan realised there was a lot more to it than he had appreciated.

Back at work he began to spend more and more time talking about Rugby with Charlie, Keith and Big Joan. It was amazing they ever found time to do any work. But Grovsy didn't appear to be bothered. Since Basil Wilkinson had assumed command, he seemed to have completely changed.

It had now sunk in that Joshua Wilkinson would not be coming back for quite some time, if at all. His eldest son, Basil, was now exerting his influence and showing them all that he was the boss. At least once a week he would come up from London to make sure his instructions were being carried out. By the time he had left, somebody or other had been affected by his visit. For some it would be an increased workload, for others it would be a telling off or an official reprimand and, in some cases, a sacking.

But nobody complained when George Hall was given his cards. Hitler, as he was usually known as behind his back, was a loud-mouth, a bully and a hypocrite, all rolled into one. He was in charge of the special projects section of the Machine Shop, where much of the firm's experimental equipment was assembled.

Inevitably a lot of the things that his men made were scrapped. On the side, George had an arrangement with a scrap metal dealer from Widnes. Every few weeks, but always on a Saturday morning, all the metal that had been dumped in the yard outside his office would be removed. It had been done that way for months.

George didn't get paid for working overtime, so he usually arrived about nine and stayed around for an hour just to show his face, and, if his luck was in, to catch

48

somebody not working. On the morning in question it was nearer to ten by the time he drove in.

Unfortunately for him Old Jack, who always collected the scrap, was ill so he had sent his son instead. He quickly loaded up the lorry and by half past nine was wanting to be away. Unable to find George in his office, he wandered into the Machine Shop and saw a lone figure prowling around.

"Hey, mate, have you seen George?"

Unknown to him, his "mate" was Basil Wilkinson doing a little inspection when no one was about.

"No, I haven't. Why? Who are you?"

"Jack's lad. I just wanted to tell him we've collected all his scrap."

"Have you got some record of what you have taken?"

"No."

"Well surely there must be some paperwork to go with it?"

"No. That's how George likes it. What the eye doesn't see, the heart doesn't grieve over. The bosses here don't need the money. They're rolling in it."

When George walked in half an hour later, Basil Wilkinson accused him of selling what didn't belong to him. He didn't have a leg to stand on.

"Don't come Monday, we'll send your cards on to you."

And without knowing it, Basil Wilkinson gave the Machine Shop an early and very welcome Christmas present.

10
CHRISTMAS EVE 1962

On the morning of Christmas Eve, Basil Wilkinson called all the managers to his office and told them that his father had decided to retire. He went on to tell them of the changes that would be necessary as a result... and then came the punchline:

"I have decided to appoint a managing director and put him in charge of the factory. He will be answerable to me and me alone. He has had a lot of experience in industry. I am sure you will all give him any help he needs. His name is Stephen Williams and he will start early in the New Year."

Then he raised his glass, wished them all the best for the coming year, and shortly after Joshua Wilkinson's eldest son returned to his big house in Surrey and his life of wining and dining important people in the City and Government.

While this news was being announced, the employees, or at least some of them, had carried on working. Then at lunch time all work came to an end. Many went out for a drink and when they returned the fun and games would begin. It was a time when a few short-lived liaisons were formed, when some employees did to other employees what they had fancied doing to them all year. Some got away with it, some didn't and some wished they had never even considered it, particularly those whose deeds or, more likely, whose mis-deeds would be remembered for years to come.

Last year it had been one of the apprentices. He had gone to the brass foundry, looking for a bit of slap and tickle with the girls who worked in the pattern shop. He was like a lamb to the slaughter. A couple were sat on the bench necking with two moulders. The rest were all hanging around, just waiting for it thought the lad knowing of their reputation. One of them, big Martha she was called, took hold of him and kissed him. Then she took hold of his hand and led him into the store room.

She kicked the door shut and said, "Have you brought me a little Christmas present, lover boy", as she began to undo the front of her smock. Quickly the lad started to take off his boots and then his boiler suit and trousers. Suddenly the other girls rushed in, pulled down his under pants and covered his private parts with engine grease, iron filings and handfuls of sand. Then they hung his trousers on the crane hook and told the crane driver to hoist them up.

The year before it had been Ronnie Garner. He had gone to see Lorna, one of the telephonists. Both had had a few drinks and one thing soon began to lead to another.

First their conversation became rather saucy and then their actions passionate. Unfortunately for them, what they didn't realise was that the switch on Lornas's control desk that she used when broadcasting messages to the factory was turned on. Any one near a loudspeaker could hear it all. When Ronnie heard about it later, he said he had only done it for a laugh and nothing had really happened. But every body knew that wasn't true. They all knew what he was like.

In the drawing office, the draughtsmen appeared to be working, but in reality not one line was added to one drawing. The first hour was spent moving bits of paper around, taking long lost drawings back to the print room and tidying up. But when Joan appeared with the tea trolley, the charade came to an end. First Grovesy produced a bottle from his 'entertainment' cupboard and Anne, who had still not got the message, gave everybody one of her teeth-shattering Sutton rock cakes.

Then John Battesby called them all together and proceeded to deliver his usual Christmas address. It was full of references to his one great passion in life, sailing. In his view the year ahead was going to be a difficult one, since Joshua Wilkinson, who he called the Great Helmsman, would no longer be navigating for them. "No longer on board, just resident in port."

"Didn't he mean whisky," quipped Yorky.

If John heard him, he didn't let on as he carried on to say that if they all pulled together like a well drilled team of oarsmen, the Drawing Office would once again lead the way. He finished, as he always did, by reminding his crew that work began every day at eight 'o' clock, not one minute past or half past. Then he wished everyone all the best, looked forward to whistling them all on board in the New Year and returned to his office. Straight away the rest of them put on their jackets and made a hasty exit. It was essential to get to The Worsley Arms before the works were let out.

They managed to get into the back room and order the first round and the food before the rush. The pub was well known for its special delicacy, meat and potato pie with chips, beans and gravy, a solid Lancashire dish that would stick to your ribs. As soon as they had all eaten, it was time for the Drawing Office awards ceremony. This year there would be six awards; the Biggest Cock up of the Year, the Daftest Statement of the Year, the Meanest Act of the Year, King Overtime, Mr. Romance and the Holder of the Golden Pencil. This was the most honoured one and went to whoever had managed to get one over on Lurch. As always special hats had been made and each winner had to wear his for the rest of the day.

Around quarter to two some began to drift back to work, hoping to sneak into a party in the General Offices. Before Alan could decide what to do, Charlie shouted out that it was about time Greenall bought some Greenalls for all those with empty glasses. As a result he was amongst the last out of the pub. By the time he got back to the office every body had gone and one of the security men was turning out the lights. It was old Joe, the miserable one. Alan had never seen him smile. "Well, all the best for Christmas old lad," he said as he grabbed his donkey jacket. He didn't wait for the reply; he knew Joe would either moan about having to work, or, if he wasn't working, about having to go to his mother-in-law's.

By half past seven he was sat in The Nags Head in Market street. With him were Ken, Roy and Geoff. Each had a story to tell about what had happened at work that day. By the time they had finished it was nine o clock and they had still not decided what they were going to do next.

"Are we going to the Co-op Hall then?" asked Alan.

"We'll never get in," replied Geoff. "It'll be packed in there by now."

"I can get us in."

"How?"

"My Uncle Stan is on the door tonight."

"I always knew you were a clever bugger. Come on then, let's get among them," said Geoff finishing his pint off in one gulp.

As they crossed the road Alan told them the way he could do it. He would go up to his uncle but pretend not to know him and say, "Have you got four tickets for Greenall?" His uncle would say no and Alan would walk away. Five minutes later the four of them would re-appear and one of the others had to ask the second doorman the same question. By this time his uncle had written the name Greenall and the figure four in the book, while his partner was not looking. He probably did the same for any of his relatives or friends. Both worked on the basis that what they had not seen they could not be blamed for.

After getting the nod from his uncle, Alan walked back to the others who had now been joined by another drunken young man. It was Eric Yates, who Alan had known for years. Alan knew that Eric would try and get in with them, but he would have no chance, not tonight. As they walked up the steps again to the entrance, Pamela, an old flame of his, lurched towards him and started kissing him. It was good while it lasted but he knew what she was really like. By the time she had let go of him the other four were in and Uncle Stan had disappeared. When he tried to get in, the other doorman stopped him.

"If you've no ticket, you can't come in."

"But I'm Greenall. There's four tickets for Greenall."

"That's right, and four have just gone in".

Then one of the two coppers on duty said "I don't care if you're Duggie Greenall. You're not coming in here tonight pal. So you might as well buzz off home."

It just wasn't worth making a fuss. There were three of them and they were all bigger than him. Slowly he walked back down the steps. Pamela had now disappeared although that was probably a good thing he thought. Despite the rain, there were people all around him, laughing, joking and shouting. It was Christmas Eve and here he was on his own. It had never been known before. He stood there not knowing what to do next when a bus pulled up right in front of him. He watched the passengers as they got off. Then he looked inside at those who had stayed on and saw a familar face. It was Thelma, who worked in the Planning Engineers office.

She was a bit of an unusual girl and many of the draughtsmen liked to make fun of her, her dress sense, or rather lack of it, her accent and her freckles. He never did. He quite liked her, although it had never crossed his mind to ask her out, partly because he thought she was courting; but then if she was courting what was she doing out on her own on Christmas Eve? He wondered if she would come for a drink with him. At least he would not finish up on his own for the rest of the evening. He waved to her, indicating with his hand that she should get off. She did, pushing past a woman with an enormous bag of shopping.

As she came towards him, he noticed she had clearly not dressed up for the evening. Same old black shoes, same old coat she always wore and that shoulder bag she took everywhere, the one with the Ban The Bomb symbol on the side. Two things were different tonight however. She was wearing a woolly hat and white ankle socks. She looked like a pixie out of a Rupert Bear story, he thought.

"Hello, Freckles. What are you doing out on your own tonight?"

"I could ask you the same question, Alan. Have all your mates deserted you?"

"Sort of. I've been messed around up there. Listen, it's too early to be going home. How do you fancy coming for a drink?"

"Alright."

"Should we go to The Raven?"

"Do you mind if we go Mario's? You look as though you've had more than enough beer for one day and I'd love a hot drink. I'm freezing. I've been waiting over half an hour for that bus."

Within five minutes they were sat in a corner seat in the town's newest coffee bar. There were quite a few people in the place but no-one paid any attention to them. He asked her what sort of a day she had had. It turned out that the engineers had stayed until lunch time and then finished. Thelma had gone with Big Joan, Rita and two of Rita's friends to the Bottle and Glass. After that they had gone to a party in the Sales Office.

As they talked he looked at her closely. She was not particularly good looking, not like Helen Murdoch or Margaret Berry, who he had gone out with for ages until she had gone to University. As always her hair was a bit of a mess. He guessed that she had once had a bad cut to her cheek bone and her eyes did not look identical. But just like when they were at work, he enjoyed talking to her, and she was certainly good company.

He tried to find what she did in her spare time. Except for going to the CND meeting once a month, she didn't seem to have much of a social life. They stopped talking for a while to watch a couple of drunks outside acting the goat for the benefit of all those in the coffee bar. When they had gone he asked her what she was doing over Christmas.

"Are you going to any parties?"

She shook her head. "No, I'm not going anywhere."

"So what are you doing tomorrow? Falling asleep in front of the fire after you've had your turkey and your Christmas pudding?"

"No. Not even that. It'll have to be something out of a tin. I'm hopeless at cooking anything."

"So, are all your family still down in Wales then?"

"No."

She paused for a moment, looked down towards the table top and continued, with her hand partly covering her mouth.

"There's only me, Alan. My mum died when I was a baby. I was brought up in a home."

He said nothing. Those few words had made an impact on him and it must have shown on his face.

"Don't look so worried, Alan," she said now bravely smiling. "As long as I've got enough shillings for the gas, I'll be fine. I've just started reading a great book. The time will fly by."

Alan was now thinking of the contrast. Tomorrow he would be at his Granny's, surrounded by all his relatives, eating, drinking and making merry. On the other hand, this poor slip of a girl would be all on her own, eating something warmed up out of a tin.

It was not just that he liked her, although he did. It was not just that he felt sorry for her, although he did. It was just not right. When he was a lot younger, whenever he read stories about orphans, it always brought tears to his eyes. The thought of some poor child having no one in the world to care for them was something that had always struck a chord within him. But he had never actually met an orphan before, and now here he was sat with one. He knew straight away what he ought to do, and it was also what he wanted to do.

"Look, Thelma. I'm not religious. You know that, but since it's Christmas, would you let me invite you somewhere?"

She was puzzled by this. Maybe it was to a party, fine, but why had he said he was not religious? Or was it to a religious event, midnight mass perhaps? She waited for him to continue.

"How would you like to spend Christmas Day with us? I'd like you to come. I'd feel bad if I thought you were going to be all on your own tomorrow with no one to talk to or have a drink with."

"Oh, Alan, thank you, but no, I couldn't come. It wouldn't be fair on your mum. Not at such short notice. She wouldn't be expecting me. It would be extra work for her. She wouldn't want that, not on Christmas Day."

"Look, it wouldn't affect my mum at all. We all go down to my Granny's. There'll be my sister and her husband and a couple of aunties and uncles. There will be eleven of us, if you count our Joan's baby. One more mouth to feed, would hardly be noticed. And we always seem to leave loads. It's criminal when you think of all the starving people in the world."

She didn't reply, and it struck Alan that she might feel uncomfortable sat at a table with so many people she did not know. Of course he knew all his relatives would go out of their way to make her feel at home, but she couldn't know that. And he was sure she didn't really want to be on her own, not on Christmas Day. So he decided to make something up, tell her a story he had once read in a book somewhere.

"Look Thelma, every year my Granny puts an empty plate on the table. She says it is for someone passing by, someone who has nowhere to go or enjoy the day. She's quite religious in her own way and she has done that for years. But that plate has always been left empty. If you came, you would really make her day and we'll all make you very welcome."

She was now fumbling with her purse. "I think I'd better go or I'll miss the last bus. How much do I owe you for the coffee?"

"Put your money away, I'll pay for this," and he walked over to the till before she could raise any objection.

He helped her on with her coat and noticed how quiet she was. As they walked down Bridge Street, he put his arm around her and told her again how much he wanted her to come. He saw that her bus had just pulled in. There wasn't much time left.

"You'll enjoy yourself Thelma. Honest. I know you will. It'll be better than being on your own all day tomorrow. And you'll really like my Granny."

It must have been those last few words that swung it. She looked up at him with her lips gripped together and nodded. Then, almost as though she was having to force the words out, as though she was being made to admit to something that she hadn't done and was to be severely punished for, she quietly said:

"Yes, I'd like to come if you're really sure it will be alright?"

55

"It will be."

"Where does she live?"

"In Silkstone Street near the Baths, but I'll come and fetch you. Where do you live?"

"Number ten, Grasmere Avenue. It's just past the butchers on Haydock Lane, up at the top."

Then she leaned forward, gave him a fleeting kiss on his cheek, and said: "Thanks Alan, and thanks for the coffee."

She sat down on the same seat she had been on earlier. It might even have been the same bus. He waved as it pulled away, and when the conductor came for her fare, he saw she was wiping tears from her eyes.

11
CHRISTMAS DAY 1962

He decided to call in at his Granny's on his way home. As he set off he saw Eric at the number fourteen bus stop with two girls from Hemsley. An hour ago he could have killed his so-called mate. Now he was beginning to feel glad about what had happened. Funny how things can change.

He walked into the house and found his grandparents drinking tea. It looked as though they had only just sat down. They had probably been running round ever since they got up. Christmas Eve was always such a busy day for them.

"Goodness me, Alan. I didn't expect to see you tonight, or have you come early for your dinner?" said his Granny.

"I'd forgotten we were coming here tomorrow."

"Forgotten my foot. That's one thing you won't forget. And where have you been all evening, I bet you've been in the pub?"

He declined the offer of a drink and proceeded to tell them how he had spent the evening. When he told them what Eric Yates had done, his Granny burst out laughing. She knew him well. A likeable rogue she always called him.

"So what did you do then?"

"I finished up in Mario's with somebody from work."

"A bit unusual for you that, isn't it? Drinking coffee when they are still serving beer."

"I'd had enough. We'd been on the ale since dinner time."

He paused for a moment and said: "Granny, can I ask you a very special favour?"

"Alan, you've been asking favours ever since you learned to talk. What is it now?"

"This friend from work, she told me that she was going to be on her own tomorrow. So I've invited her to come here for her dinner. Do you mind? Is it all right?"

"So you've got yourself a young lady have you? You've kept that quiet from your old Granny. And why didn't you take her to the Co-op Hall? I'm sure you would rather dance with her than Geoff Platt."

"I'm not going out with her. She's just a friend."

"Of course she's welcome. You should know that. I've never turned any of your friends away, and that includes Mr. Scruffy Pants Yates."

"I know, but Christmas Day is a bit different."

"It doesn't matter."

"She doesn't smoke a pipe or belch at the table does she?" asked Grandad wryly.

Granny laughed and asked, "Where does she come from, Alan?"

"Wales, but she lives in Grasmere Avenue now."

"And where are all her family. Don't they live there?"

"I didn't know before tonight, but she hasn't got any. Her mother died when she was a baby and she was brought up in a home. I don't really know a lot more about her."

"Well that settles it. She can come for her dinner by all means, and her tea. She can stay for her supper as well if she wants to."

"Thanks Granny. I knew it would be alright. But will there be enough room? We can eat in the kitchen if we have to."

"No, it's alright, there'll be plenty room. Your Auntie Hilda and Uncle Eric aren't coming. They've gone down with the flu. Anyway, what's her name?"

"Thelma."

"Thelma. That's a nice name. And from Welsh Wales too. Well I am looking forward to meeting her."

"She's very nice. I'm sure you'll like her."

"I'm sure I will."

"Does she play the harp?" interrupted Grandad again.

"Behave yourself Ned. And don't you be trotting out that tale about when you and Bob went to Portmadoc. Whatever will she think of us if you start telling her about things like that."

As he walked home the rain was now turning to snow. Maybe it was going to be a white Christmas. He felt good about the way things had finally turned out. He had always got on well with her at work, despite what the others said about her. She had always been good to talk to, although a bit of a mystery. Now he was beginning to understand why, and when she had told him that she was going to be on her own all over Christmas, well there was only one thing to do and he had done it. He was looking forward to tomorrow even more now, though it was a pity Auntie Hilda wouldn't be there. She was always the life and soul of the party.

By the time Thelma arrived home she was wet through. She quickly turned on the gas fire and was soon sat drinking cocoa. She was now wearing her pyjamas, the old dressing gown she had brought from the home and an even older pair of slippers. Usually, she would get out her latest library book and become oblivious to the world outside. But not tonight.

While she had been at her friend's house up Nook End, they had drunk half a bottle of sherry between them and had a good laugh. She had played with the baby and promised to come again if she could find the time. She had led Beryl to believe that lots of people from work had invited her to call round over the holidays. If only Beryl knew that Thelma had been making it all up. After she had left the house she had stood outside Nook End Labour club for ages waiting for the bus back into town. She saw all the people going inside and felt lonely. She wished she could be part of a group going out having a good time somewhere. But she knew that until she went back to work she would be on her own.

She had been living in Ashurst since May. She liked it up North and found Lancashire people very friendly and easy to get on with. But it always takes time to become settled in a place where you began by knowing virtually no one. She remembered somone telling her that the best way to get to know lots of people and make friends in a new place was to join as many organisations as she could. But that is easier said than done. After two months the only thing she had joined was the library. She went there every week and soon struck up a friendship with one of the librarians. It was through her that she went to her first CND meeting in the Quaker Hall.

After she had been going for a few weeks, one of the young men convinced her that she should be in the Labour Party. So she let him take her to North Ashurst Labour Club and that night she joined the Young Socialists. At the time there was a bitter struggle going on between Keep Left and Militant for control of the branch. She didn't fully understand the major issues or the differences between them and so joined neither side. Then when the clever one, the one who had an answer for everything, began to call her a wishy washy liberal and an enemy of the working class she stopped going. If only any of them knew what sort of a background she had come from.

She was so pleased that she was not going to be on her own on Christmas Day. She had always wanted to be part of a large family, to have a brother and a sister, uncles, aunties, grandparents, cousins and of course a mum and dad. But fate had decreed that she would have none. Now she was going to spend the day with somebody else's family. Neither was it any old family, good as that might be. It was Alan's family, Alan who she had liked ever since she first set eyes on him in the print room. She couldn't believe her good fortune.

She went into her bedroom. Little Ted was there as always. He had been with her as long as she could remember. He had been her main source of comfort so many times in a cruel world. It was amazing he had not died of pneumonia the number of times he had been drenched by her tears. The room was cold but it didn't matter. Within five minutes she was fast asleep and as usual little Ted had fallen on the floor.

It was nearly nine when she woke up. By ten o clock she was ready for her big day. She was so excited. She looked out of the window. It was pelting down. She didn't think the weather would put him off. No, she was sure that he would come. He had said he would, less than twelve hours ago. But then he had had a lot to drink and she also remembered that others in the past had promised to do things for her and then let her down. But she was sure he wouldn't.

Perhaps he would go to see his Granny first to make sure it was alright. She might say yes but then she might have to say there wasn't enough room. But then what had he said about that empty plate she always put on the table. And if he did have to tell her that his Granny had said sorry for whatever reason, perhaps he just might ask if he could take her out some time. She could survive a lonely Christmas if she had a date with him to look forward to.

She brushed her hair for the fourth time and tidied the room. Below the sink one of the cupboard doors was open. She saw the tins all stood there in a row.

"You've all been given a reprieve. I won't be having any of you today," she said to them, but under her breath she muttered the words "I hope".

It was now nearly one and there was still no sign of him. She began to fear the worst. The gas fire started spluttering. She took a shilling off the mantelpiece and put it in the meter. If he didn't come soon he wouldn't come at all. She blinked back a tear and walked to the window again. There wasn't a soul in sight, not surprising seeing how bad the weather had now become.

She went upstairs to the front bedroom. Same sight, same weather, same absence of human life. She went into her own room and looked at the houses opposite. It was raining just as much there. She sat on the bed and glanced at some of the people who always kept an eye on her: James Dean, Sal Mineo, William Holden, Bill Haley and Jack Palance among others. Then she picked up Little Ted and sat him on her knee.

"It looks like I'm going to be staying here today Little Ted. I don't think he's going to come. I thought he would. He said he would. I was really looking forward to a nice Christmas dinner. You wouldn't have minded, would you?"

He indicated that it would have been alright by him if she had gone out for the day, as long as she didn't leave him lying on the floor. He always agreed with whatever she said. He was such a good friend. Wherever would she have been without him all these years.

She stroked his head and thanked him for the present he had given her for Christmas. She asked him if he liked what she had given him. He had. It was a large bar of chocolate and later on they would share it together. She sat there idly swinging her legs and looking round the half furnished room. Life hadn't been too kind to her, but she knew that there were lots of people much worse off than her. She wondered what he would say when he saw her again after the holidays. Maybe he would say he was sorry, really sorry. Perhaps he had just forgotten the number, he was still pretty drunk when she had told him.

60

And then she heard a familiar noise, that little squeak as the garden gate opened. Somebody was coming to the house. She waited with baited breath for what seemed an eternity. Then she heard a knock on the front door. She rushed down the stairs, stopped for a moment to catch her breath, and then slowly peeped round the corner. She saw his face through the frosted glass. He had come. She knew he would.

"Happy Christmas, Thelma, sorry I'm late. I've had to keep sheltering."

He briefy brushed his lips across her cheek as she let him into the house. He sat down on the old settee and ran his hands across his wet face. He glanced around the room as she stood there waiting to hear her fate. She could hardly stand the tension. It was almost too much to bear. She looked at him, her hands behind her back and her fingers tightly crossed, just hoping he was going to say it was alright. He wiped his mouth with the back of his hand and explained:

"I went to my Granny's after I left you last night. Do you know what she said when I told her about you?"

Thelma didn't know. How could she. But she was soon going to and it was good news, in fact the best news she had had for a very long time.

"She said that you'll be very welcome. You can come for your dinner and your tea. You can even stay for your supper if you want to."

She couldn't believe it. There must be a catch in it somewhere she thought. She wished there weren't going to be so many relatives to be introduced to. But that was a lot better than not going at all. And what had he said last night, "You'll really like my Granny." Well now she was going to meet her. She wondered what she was like.

As she put her coat on, she nervously commented that it looked as though they were going to get wet.

"We won't. My Uncle Stan is going to pick us up. He always ferries everybody about on Christmas Day."

And almost as though someone up above was writing the script, there was a toot, toot outside. Thelma's stagecoach had arrived in the shape of Ashurst Corporation Plumbing Department's Works van.

They ran from the house and climbed into the back. Any conversation was well nigh impossible since the exhaust was just about ready to fall off. Within minutes they were nearly there.

Alan's mum who had been sat in the front, asked her brother to stop. "I want to see Mrs. Freeman. Don't wait for me. I'll walk down," and with a special smile for Thelma she got out.

They were dropped off at the top of Silkstone Street and Uncle Stan drove off to pick up more relatives. Alan and Thelma were the first to enter the house. As soon as they walked into the living room, Granny scurried in from the kitchen to greet them.

"Hello, Thelma. I am very pleased to meet you. You are very welcome love."

Thelma could tell straight away that her words were sincere. She liked the way Lancashire people used the word love at the end of their sentences. It was more than a simple four letter word. It expressed a whole attitude to life, one that indicated that we are all equals on this earth, so let's be friends and get on together.

Grandad came in from the yard and was introduced. Then Granny asked: "Can you and Alan go and borrow a couple of chairs from Mrs. Higham. You'll have to go round the back. There's something wrong with her front door."

Then, turning back to Thelma, she said "Let's have your coat, love."

As it was being hung up, Thelma said: "Can I do anything to help, Mrs. Greenall?"

"Come in the kitchen first and see what a fine bird we've got," and as she spoke, she put her hand on Thelma's arm, smiled and said, "Just call me Granny".

They looked at the turkey roasting away in the oven surrounded by potatoes, carrots and parsnips. Then, as she carried on putting the final touches to the meal, she talked to her young guest. Alan was certainly right when he had told Thelma that she would like his Granny. By the time the other relatives arrived they were chattering away as though they had known each other for years. She had also drunk a large sherry and felt quite relaxed. When she came out of the kitchen to be introduced to everybody it was nowhere near as bad as she had first feared.

The seating arrangements were planned so that she sat between Alan and Granny. She soon polished off her dinner and didn't take much persuading to have a second helping. This was followed by an enormous piece of Christmas pudding and a couple of mince pies. To finish off with, she had a cup of coffee laced with brandy. She hardly said a thing all the time they were eating, but each time he looked at her she had that smile on her face, her cheeks were flushed and her eyes were sparkling. She had had to wait until she was turned nineteen to enjoy her first family Christmas dinner. It would appear to have been worth waiting for.

After Auntie Doris and his sister Joan had done the washing up, it was time for the games. In the past when there had been children present and this had been a time of great hilarity. More recently it had been a time for chatting. But today was just like the old days. Having lost her early nervousness, and fortified by the sherry and the brandy, Thelma began to join in the games with a vengeance. If she realised what a noise she was making she would have put a plaster over her mouth. But nobody minded. They could see how she was enjoying herself.

"Look at the time, and we haven't had the horse race game yet," exclaimed Granny." Let's give the presents out and then it'll be time for tea."

Thelma went quiet for she knew this part of the day wouldn't involve her. She didn't mind. She was really enjoying just being there with so many friendly people in front of a big roaring fire. Uncle Jack always did the honours. He would pick a present from under the tree, give it out and at the same time announce who it was from. He had nearly finished when he lifted up a small package, gave it to Thelma and announced:

"This is from Granny."

She unwrapped it slowly, conscious that they were all watching her. It was a pocket diary for 1963 and had almost certainly been bought for somebody else. She looked up at Granny, muttered thank you, then rushed across the room and ran up the stairs. Alan made a move to follow her to see what was wrong but his mum restrained him.

"Leave her a few minutes, Alan. I think she might have been overwhelmed by it all today. It's probably been a bit too much for her."

Everyone began to say how well she had done and what a nice girl she was. After a few minutes Granny got up from her chair and slowly went upstairs to find out what was wrong. She found her young guest crying on the bathroom floor.

"I'm sorry. I'm sorry. I couldn't help it. You've all been so nice to me. I've never been to anything like this before. I'm sorry I've gone and spoiled it. I'm sorry."

It was the culmination of a lot of things. The nerves and needless worry that morning, the strain of meeting so many new people, the rich food she was not used to and the quantity of it, drinking too much the night before, a large sherry before dinner and the brandy after it. And if this was the first time she had ever been to a family Christmas Day dinner, it was not suprising it had affected her. Granny led her into the back room and helped her lie down on the spare bed. She stroked her brow and talked softly to her and told her not to worry about it.

Granny could well appreciate how the poor girl must be feeling. Her mother had died when she was in her early teens, but at least she had been part of a large family. When Thelma had lost her mother, she had no other relative in the world. No matter how well she may have been looked after by others in the home, it was no substitute. And obviously what had happened today had been just that bit too much for her.

While this was going on, the others began to lay the table for tea. Around this time there would be a few changes. Auntie Doris and Uncle Jack would go off to their son's house in Earlestown. Alan's brother Paul would soon arrive along with his wife Dorothy and their children Michael and Paul. They had eaten their Christmas dinner at Dorothy's mother's house in Kenyon Street. And as Auntie Doris left, she said to Alan, probably for the fifth time, what a nice girl Thelma was and to bring her round to their house when she was better.

After they had gone, Granny told Alan to go and see how she was. He found her in the bathroom where she had been sick. She had eaten too much and she had drunk too much. On top of that she had been drenched going home from work three nights on the trot, and although she didn't know it then, had the flu coming on. She had so much wanted to enjoy the day and make a good impression on Alan and his family. Now all she wanted to do was be on her own, away from them all. She could have done that just as easily in that half furnished bedroom in Grasmere Avenue.

But if she had fallen ill there, she wouldn't have been kept warm by a hot brick wrapped in cloth, nor offered an endless procession of drinks. And she most certainly would not have had the undivided loving care and attention of an old lady whose existence she did not even know about less than twenty four hours earlier.

"I'm not having her going back to an empty house. She is staying here tonight. And if she's no better in the morning, I'll have to call the doctor out."

And that is what Granny had to do. Poor Thelma. Her big day spoiled. She always knew that he would turn up and he had. Then once she had got over her early nervousness, well really from the moment she had set eyes on his Granny, she had begun to enjoy her Christmas Day. It all seemed to be going so well and then this. It was just not how she had hoped the day would end. Life just didn't seem to be fair. And whatever would happen now.

12
THE BIG FREEZE

He lay in bed thinking about the day ahead. The major sporting event of the holiday period, some would say the whole year, was in prospect, the clash between St. Helens and Wigan at Knowsley Road. He was meeting the others at twelve. They aimed to get to the ground early. A full house was expected. They would be back in town around five, in good time to go to Auntie Doris's for tea. That was where all the relatives would reassemble, along with Auntie Polly who was ninety-four. After that it was down to Seddon Avenue, where the Parr household were having a do. It looked like being a hectic day.

But first he would go down to Silkstone Street and see how Thelma was. He had now decided that she would figure in his plans for the evening. Yesterday Auntie Doris had told him to bring her round any time. Well there was no time like the present, so why not tonight. And after that he'd take her to Ken's party.

He opened the curtains and saw that it was snowing. When he looked down at the ground he realised that it must have been snowing all night. It was at least two feet deep and nearly five feet against next door's shed where it had drifted. He watched it worsen as he ate his breakfast. By the time he left the house it was blowing a blizzard. "I bet it gets called off", he said to himself as he struggled down Parry Lane. It was, and the next time St. Helens played was at Craven Park in East Hull on the ninth of March. The big freeze that would totally disrupt the rest of the 1962/63 season had begun.

As soon as he walked into the house, he was greeted with the news that the doctor had just left. Thelma was very poorly and would have to stay in bed for at least a week.

"I'm sorry about this Granny," he said as he warmed himself in front of the fire.

"There's nothing to be sorry about, Alan. She's just fallen ill. It's not her fault is it. I'm sure she didn't want to".

"I know, but it's going to spoil your Christmas isn't it?"

"It wouldn't be the first time one of you lot has been sick on Christmas Day."

"Yes, I know, but we were all your relatives."

"And you were all very lucky. This poor girl, she hasn't got one relative in the world. It's the very least we can do for her. You don't think I would send her out in this, do you."

"So you don't mind having her here then."

"Of course I don't mind. She's a nice girl. A bit quiet at first maybe, but she did very well yesterday."

Then she continued: "Doctor Jackson said that she is very run down and underweight. Whoever is she living with, Alan. I bet she's not eating properly or enough, poor thing. The way she ate yesterday, you would think she hadn't eaten for weeks."

"She told me she was hopeless at cooking."

"Well, we'll get her better first and then we'll see if we can fatten her up a bit."

Alan knew what that meant: broth, hot pot, spare ribs with lentils, scouse, lobbies, stew and dumplings. What a treat was in store for her, if only she knew it. And then there would be his Grandad's famous pancakes, the ones that were sometimes found stuck to the ceiling.

"Can I go up and see her?"

"Yes, but don't wake her if she's asleep. She was up half the night. And after that you'd better go down to her house and tell whoever lives there that she is going to be staying here for a bit. And bring back some of her clothes. I've got her sleeping in one of your Grandad's shirts. Hardly very ladylike is it?"

He went up to her bedroom. She was as white as the pillow. Even her freckles were off colour. Her eyes remained closed as he stroked her brow and held her hand. He smiled to himself when he thought what Charlie would say if he could see them now:

"He's only been going out with her for a day and he's got her into bed already."

He stayed for a while, trying to put some warmth in her cold hand and then left. He struggled across town to Grasmere Avenue. It was a good job he had taken her front door key from her handbag. Whoever else lived in the house had clearly not been there since yesterday. He left a note on the table to say where she was staying and went upstairs to get some of her clothes. It didn't take long, she didn't seem to have that many. He looked around her rather bare room. He recognised a few familiar faces on the wall: James Dean, Sal Mineo, Jack Palance, Tony Curtis and Dickie Valentine. As he turned to leave he saw a rag doll on the bed. He put it in his bag. No doubt it was important to her, just like Straw Man had once been to him.

On his way back, he saw various people he knew struggling through the snow. Everybody told him what was now fairly obvious, the match was off. Thelma was still asleep when he got back so he left the doll on her pillow. He kissed her on the cheek but she did not respond. She was like a block of ice.

He came downstairs to a plate of turkey sandwiches and a big mug of tea. It was clear now that Granny would not be going to Auntie Doris's in the afternoon. There was no way she would be leaving her charge even if she could have got out of the

66

house. For the next few days, weeks if necessary, she would look after her patient as though she was a new born baby. Of course it was a real pity Thelma had fallen ill. But he knew that she couldn't have chosen a better place to do it. There was nothing he could do. Granny had it all under control so he offered to walk down to Rivington Avenue and tell Auntie Doris what had happened.

When he arrived he found Auntie Polly there and in fine form. She wasn't going to let a bit of snow spoil her Boxing Day. "All the more medicine for me," she laughed as she waved her glass of Birch wine in the air. And of course it wasn't long before she started telling him about what winters were like when she was a girl. He'd heard them all before, especially about the winter of 1879, but he didn't mind. She was good to listen to, even if she did keep repeating herself. By the time he finally arrived home he was exhausted. He felt like Scott of the Antartic trudging through the snow and within half an hour he was fast asleep.

He went back to work the next day. As he walked into the office, he saw Joe Cunningham talking to Charlie. Joe was an installation engineer and worked most of the time out on site. Every month he would spend a day in the office, going through the drawings, indicating all the cock-ups he had found, getting his next trip organised and amusing them with his tales.

After a while he walked over and sat on Alan's reference table.

"So, when's the big day, Greeno?"

"What big day?"

"Your wedding day."

How could Joe know so soon what had happened over Christmas. He lived in Daresbury Road in Eccleston, on the far side of St. Helens. Surely the news hadn't travelled so far already.

"I didn't know I was getting married."

"Have I put my foot in it or am I the carrier of bad news."

"Joe, what are you on about?"

"I was at my sister's on Christmas Eve and that bus conductress you were going out with the last time I was here was there. She lives next door. After she had gone I said to our Mary that she was putting on a fair bit of weight. Now this may come as a bit of a shock to you. Maybe I should have kept my big mouth shut. She said that's because she's having a baby. Did you not know. Eh, I'm sorry, old lad."

"It's not me, Joe, that's for sure. I never went out with her. I did my ankle in that afternoon."

Shortly after he asked Keith if he knew anything about it. He didn't, but a few weeks later at Sacred Heart church, Helen Murdoch became Helen Hurst, and on June the twentieth 1963, she gave birth to Rachael Margaret Hurst, eight and a half months after the day she should have met Alan outside the Gas Showrooms.

On his way back he called in the Print Room. Big Joan and Rita were talking to Tony Cropper, a planning engineer.

"Brian is going to be off for a fortnight," he heard Tony say, "and Roy's wife has rung to say he won't be in either. Thelma is off as well. I'm sure she was due back today."

"What was she doing over the holidays, Joan?" asked Rita.

"She was going to her friend's at Nook End on Christmas Eve. I think she said she was going to a couple of parties as well. Have you seen her on your travels round town, Greeno?"

He had to tell them all some time. It might as well be now, and by the time he had finished Len and Dickie were listening as well.

"She was always so secretive about her family," said Rita. "No wonder, she didn't have one, poor kid."

"I always knew something was wrong, but I never liked to ask her too many questions. She would always change the subject whenever you asked her anything about herself," said Joan. "To be honest, I thought she had run away from something or someone."

The news quickly went round and before long a large get well card was purchased which dozens of people signed. Then a box of chocolates appeared which Joan decided she would take to Silkstone Street on her way home.

Except for Yorky singing "We"ll keep a Welcome in the Hillsides", no one said anything funny about it. They began calling her by her proper name, instead of the various nicknames she had been given, Freckles, Ban the Bomb and, cruelly, the little Welsh Dresser. It was amazing how many asked after her and told Alan to send her their best wishes. Whether it was because she was ill, or because she had no family, it didn't really matter. It seemed to have an immediate effect on the whole office and helped contribute to a week of peace and harmony among them. But all this was soon to be shattered by the arrival of the new Managing Director, Mr. Stephen Williams.

On his first day he called the managers to his office one by one. None seemed happy with what he told them. By Wednesday he was ready to start running the place in line with what Basil wanted. At his first meeting with John Barker, the Works Progress manager, he was told of a delay with a control panel that was due on Liverpool docks on Friday morning. He decided to go to the Wiring shop and sort it out. The foreman, Bill Kelly, explained the problem, minimising the errors that could be attributed to his men and maximising those that could be placed elsewhere.

According to Bill, one of the drawings had been altered after they had started work. This had set them back two days. The relays were difficult to connect due to the way they had been shown on the assembly drawing, and thirdly, the night shift had misunderstood the notes that Charlie had left for them. From what he heard, Mr. Williams soon concluded that the drawing office was at fault. However, Bill was well known for blaming everybody other than himself or his lads. Even if there was only one mistake on a drawing that showed the connection of over five hundred wires, his answer was always the same:

"The drawing's wrong."

Mr. Williams had dealt with draughtsmen before. In his view they were a load of piss artists or Bolshy bastards, most of them anyway. He had had his fill of them over the years. They always had a clever answer as to why the job couldn't be done the way he wanted or when he wanted it. He decided that he would go straight up there and find out who was to blame.

The first thing he saw was Mick on the phone wearing no more than his vest, underpants and socks. What Mr. Williams didn't know was that Mick had just come back from the foundry. Whenever he went there, he changed into some old clothes he kept under his reference table. He had just taken his trousers off when the phone had rung, so he had gone over to answer it.

Charlie had the window open and was holding a long wooden pole on the end of which was a piece of bread. He was feeding Harold Long, the office seagull. It was called that because it was the spitting image of the storeman in the Welding Shop.

Yorky and Elaine appeared to be dancing. Actually they were looking at one of his drawings, but he was trying to get her to move towards the end of the table under which Tony was sat with the water pistol and toy trumpet his little brother had been given at Christmas. The entry of Mr. Williams coincided with Tony's decision to fire. Elaine screamed as the water trickled down her leg. Everybody went silent when they saw who had walked in, except for Tony, who then blew loudly on the trumpet.

While this was going on, Alan and Len had their heads down. At first glance it appeared that they were the only ones working. Closer inspection revealed that they were doing their pools. Mr. Williams must have thought the office party was still going on. No one had yet taken down the Christmas decorations. He stormed out back to his office and told his secretary, the cold fish Miss Place, to find John Battesby.

The general consensus was that they had just met the new Managing Director. It was felt a more formal introduction would come later. Charlie opened a book on how long it would be before the first one was told off. It would probably be next week when their illustrious Admiral of the Fleet sailed back from visiting his auntie in Birkenhead.

The next contact Mr. Williams was due to have with the staff was at half past two when he was meeting the foremen in the Refinery. There he intended to inform them

69

of his plans and impress on them the important role they would have to play. After that he was meeting the Staff Association to tell them they were doing a wonderful job and that for them his door was always. Finally he would see the shop stewards and let them know that he didn't like unions and for them the party was over.

Rumours of what he was like had already begun to circulate. From what had been heard of him, his style of dealing with people left a lot to be desired. He would appear to have the same degree of charm as Basil. And as always the foremen were in a difficult position, caught between the management and the shop floor.

Brian Burke was in charge of the welding shop. He knew that to get to the refinery, Mr. Williams would have to walk along the alley way behind his office.It was a real eyesore. There was not much he could do about the phosopher bronze castings stacked against the walls. But the place needed tidying up. He organised two labourers to clear away the rubbish. Neither paid any attention to six wooden boxes piled up against the emergency doors.

When he returned from his lunch, they were still there. He told one of them to get the fork lift truck and move them out of sight. But Pete only ever worked at one speed, dead slow. By five past two he had only moved one box. As he started to load the second one, Brian told him to work faster and to put two boxes on. Pete protested that it was only wide enough for one.

"Get out of the way. I'll drive the bloody thing. We're not taking them to China." He revved up the engine and set off. Unfortunately one casting was sticking out about six inches more than the others. He swerved to avoid it, skidded and hit one on the other side. This fell over onto the next one and like dominoes they all toppled over. At the bottom of the alleyway were four large containers. Each of these went down as well, the lids opened spilling paint all over the place.

Roger Ellison was the youngest of the foremen. He had achieved promotion by being a creep. Telling tales, speaking posh and agreeing with what ever any manager said to him had helped his career enormously. When he heard of the meeting he had his white overalls specially washed for the occasion. He always wore a hard hat no matter where he went in the factory. He thought it made him look dignified. He really looked the part as he set off for the meeting. However, unknown to him, while he had been in the wash room, one of his girls had put a handful of red powder underneath the leather strapping inside his hat. Due to the shaky nature of his walk and the heat rising from his head, the inevitable happened. By the time he had reached the refinery, it was difficult to know whether he had red hair or blonde hair.

Mr. Pickles, made a brief speech welcoming their new boss and then proceeded to introduce each of the foremen. Norman Burrows was first. He looked after the manufacture of all the small components in the Works Production Shop. He believed

70

that every one had their chosen place in society from the day they were born. He demanded respect from those below him and gave it in a most deferential way to those above him. As Mr. Williams approached, he held out his hand, bowed to almost ninety degrees and announced he was "Burrows, Small Parts, Sir."

John Kay was next in line. He was definitly located at the opposite end of the social scale. He had once been a foreman in the Pattern shop. Now he only looked after three labourers in the Sand Wash. He should not have been present. Miss Place had used an out of date list when sending out the invitations. This explained why he was there and half of those who should have been weren't. John didn't talk much because he was having trouble with his false teeth. They just kept slipping out. As Mr. Williams approached him, they did it again. He took the top set out, wiped them on the back of his hand, put them back and then offered his wet hand to the new boss.

The next in line was Tony Sankey, the hand shaker. He was well know for it. Once he grasped Mr. Williams hand, he would not let go until he had told him his name, where he worked, what he did and how long he had been there. And all the time he was talking his hand would be going up and down.

Then came Tommy Litherland, a chargehand from the Refinery standing in for his foreman who was off sick. Tommy always referred to anybody he met as Boss. As Mr. Williams managed to prise his hand out of Tony Sankey's vice-like grip, Tommy tapped his head with two fingers, like he always did, and said, "Hi, boss. I'm Tommy Litherland. I work in here."

The last one in the line was Roger Ellison. It was quite warm in the refinery and he kept wiping his hand across his brow. When Mr. Williams saw him he said to himself, "Who the hell is this? He looks like a clown." He shook Roger's hand, then walked back to the table where he had left his papers. When he picked them up he saw that his hand was covered in red dye.

"If these are the foremen what are the rest of them like," he thought to himself as he returned to his office. He was soon to find out.

13
LANCASHIRE 6
YORKSHIRE 1

Basil had said that the new boss had had a lot of experience in industry. Well he had, on paper. He had worked for three large companies, but only in their head offices in Central London. He had certainly never worked in a place like Wilkinson's, or lived in a town like Ashurst. Not suprisingly, his first few days were something of a culture shock. And if he had been in the Foundry on the following morning, he would hardly have believed what he saw.

It was the day that old Seth went past the point of no return, the day when it became obvious that he should never be allowed to drive the big crane again. Sat up in his cabin all day, it was Seth's job to move the moulding boxes around from where the moulders first worked on the pattern to where the final castings were finished off. He had been there since the year dot, but as he grew older he began to play stupid tricks.

Every now and again, he would drive the crane hook at about four feet off the floor forcing every one to kneel or lie down on the sand. Other times he would attach a container of water to the hook and spray everybody within its range. Over the last few weeks he had taken to dropping a moulding box on the large pile of sand at the top end of the shop whenever a large delivery had just been made. This would shower the whole place and cover everyone in the stuff.

On the day in question he had had a row with one of the moulders. Seth waited until he saw the lad on his own. Then he drove at him with the aim of knocking him over and teaching him a lesson. He missed, the lad saw him coming and avoided what would have been a very nasty accident. He swore at old Seth and threw a bolt at him. This was the last straw. Seth proceeded to drive the crane up and down the shop at breakneck speed. Everybody scattered and ran to the ends of the shop where the crane did not reach. Billy Flynn, the charge-hand, saved the situation by turning the main isolator off, but when he tried to climb the stairs to Seth's cabin, the old man began throwing things at him and at anybody else he could see.

All went quiet for a few minutes before the foreman was found. As he went up the steps, Seth started shouting. A few of the moulders were now stood below looking up at him. Suddenly Seth unzipped his trousers and urinated over them all. He was finally removed from his cabin and taken straight to the medical centre from where an ambulance took him away, ultimately to Winwick mental hospital.

Two weeks later the work force was reduced in number again when a labourer walking past Roger Ellison's office dropped dead. Mr Williams had been nearby when he saw people gathering round. As he walked over to see what had happened, a first aid man came running up. He felt his pulse, felt under his chin and declared: "It's no good, he's dead." Everyone went silent until Roger told one of his assembly men to go and clock him off.

The onset of the bad weather that was to hit the country for the next ten weeks had begun on Christmas Day. Things gradually got worse and by the time they were all back at work, the whole of South Lancashire was covered in deep snow and raging Siberian style blizzards had become commonplace.

The evening of the first Thursday of 1963 was particularly bad. The following day they all had a tale to tell on how they had managed to get to work. Some, like Mick, who lived at Platt Bridge in Wigan, never made it. Dickie arrived at nine o clock and Charlie twenty minutes later. Alan was late as well, but that was nothing new, timekeeping was never one of his strong points.

After they had all settled down and started work, they were joined by Ray Birchall a section leader from the top end of the office. He had come to discuss with Len a job they had recently started at Eggborough power station in Yorkshire. After they had sorted out the main points Len asked who was going to do the detail drawings.

"I've put John Meredith on it, and if he needs any assistance, Billinge can help him."

"Why do you always call him Billinge? What's wrong with his proper name?"

"I don't know Stan. He's always been called that, ever since I've known him. I suppose it's because he comes from Billinge."

"But you don't call Mick, Platt Bridge. You don't call Dickie, Gillarsfield, do you? Why him?"

"I don't know, force of habit I suppose, but then you all call Sam, Yorky. It's only the same isn't it?"

"I would've thought it fairly obvious why he's called Yorky, among other things."

"No longer. If it's good enough for Barry Littler, it's good enough for me. From now on I want to be called Mytholmroyd."

"And from now on I want to be called Chisnall Avenue."

"I can see I'll get no more sense out of you lot today. I'm off for my bacon butty."

As they sat drinking their tea, comparisons began to be made with what things had been like in the past. Len talked about playing football on Mill Dam in 1947, and Charlie told them how he and half their street had helped dig a train out of the snow

73

at Thatto Heath. Then Dickie told them how cold it had been in Korea, but as usual Yorky managed to get the last word in. The moment he said, "I remember when I was on that Artic run", they all knew he would beåt everybody else's story. It was true. During the war he had been on convoys taking supplies up to the Russian port of Murmansk.

Then he put his cup on Joan's trolley and said, "Would any of you kind Lancashire folk like to help a war hero today?" There was a stony response. They knew from the way he said it that it would involve going out into the works somewhere.

"Would any Red Rose people like to help the White Rose on a little job?"

"For the third and last time, does anybody feel like giving me a bit of help?"

"Right then, none of you can say you weren't given a chance."

"What the hell are you on about?" said Dickie."Is every body from Yorkshire as daft as you? Has your brain got frost bite?"

"Well, Greeno, it looks as though you have just drawn the short straw. You'll be helping me today. Lucky you."

Alan groaned. It must mean it would be a donkey jacket, scarf and gloves job.

"Today you and me are going to the Rolling Mill. We have to check all the wiring in Unit Seven Control Panel, the one that's about twelve foot from the furnace."

The rest of them realised he had fooled them. If they had known where he was going, they would have all offered to help.

"That looks like Yorkshire one Lancashire nil. Come on Greeno. Let's be off to where it's nice and warm."

"However did you manage this on today of all days?" asked Alan as they hurried down through the Winding shop to the Rolling Mill.

"Easy. I told Ronnie Garner I needed to check the wiring before I can start the drawings for that new Circuit Breaker. He said to do it when it was convenient. It's called using your brain. It's what us Yorkshire folk are good at."

It was warm by the time they had climbed up to the first floor, level sixteen where the offices and electricians' cabin were located. The shift foreman was Billy Tunstall, an old friend of Yorky's. Before they had reached his office he had the kettle on and was dragging an extra chair from the store room next door.

"So, to what do we owe the honour of this visit? Don't tell me, you've come to do a heat check on the furnace?"

"No, we've come to look in Unit Seven Panel. It's purely a coincidence it's in such a nice warm spot."

"Who said Yorkshire folk were thick, this one's got his head screwed on right," Billy said to Alan. "Well, you can go up there but not before eleven. I've got an electrician working in there. You'll have to wait."

74

"Do you know, Alan? Have you had the misfortune to cross his path?"

"Yes, I remember him when he worked in here for a bit as an apprentice. You've not gone all hoity toity have you, now that you are in the drawing office?"

"No. Why do you ask that?"

"I was driving past the Baths on Christmas Day when I saw you and a young woman getting out of your Uncle Stan's van. I waved to you but you just looked straight through us."

"I can't remember. Do you know my Uncle Stan?"

"I do. We were big mates at school but I hardly ever see him these days. How is he?"

"Champion."

"And how's your Granny and Grandad? I take it you were going there for your Christmas dinner."

"Yes. We always go there on Christmas Day."

"And who was the girl? She looked familiar."

"Thelma out of the Planning Engineer's office."

"And she's still there," said Yorky.

So then Alan had to tell the whole story going right back to Christmas Eve. Billy listened with interest as Alan told him what had happened.

"Well, I'm sure she couldn't be in better hands than where she is now," he said. "I hope she appreciates it."

"I'm sure she does," said Alan. "She really is a nice kid."

"When she's better, why don't you bring her out to our place. The wife will be pleased to meet her. She's from Wales as well, near Swansea. Make a day of it. We'll take you round all the local beauty spots."

"That should take up the best part of twenty minutes."

"Eh Sam, don't you knock Leigh. It's a great place, and it's very well positioned. Do you know you can get to anywhere in the world from Leigh bus station."

The banter carried on. Billy had no intention of leaving his office, Yorky and Alan had no inclination to do any more than bask in the general warmth of the place for as long as possible. It was at times like this, being paid to listen to workmates talking, that life seemed so good. Then Billy told them how he had spent Christmas.

"We were going to visit Vera's folks but she wasn't feeling too good, so we finished up at our Frank's instead. I like going to South Wales, but not in weather like this."

Then he went on to say they always went down whenever there was a big game.

"I saw Wales play Scotland there last year. There was a big group of us went from their village, her da, three brothers, and a couple of neighbours. They all thought it was a great game, but I was'nt impressed with it. On the way home I said to her dad, you'll have to come up North and see one of our big matches.

"'How often do you get a game as good as that?'" he asked. "Every week, I said. They wouldn't believe me when I told them there was more passing and running with the ball at an 'A' team game than we'd just seen."

They were interrupted for a few minutes by one of the handlers from the Rolling Mill. After he had left Yorky said, "He's not from round here, by the sound of him."

"That's Pavel Pavlovitch," replied Alan. He used to live in the same street as one of the lads in our class."

"He's Ukranian," said Billy, "he came here after the War."

"Didn't the Nazis murder all his family?" asked Alan.

"They did. He was lucky they didn't kill him as well."

"Why, what happened?" asked Yorky.

Billy leaned back on his chair and went on: "It was when he was a kid. I think he said he was about twelve. He and a couple of his pals had been out catching rabbits in the woods. As they were going home they saw smoke in the distance. When they reached the top of the hill that overlooked their village they saw that the whole place was on fire. It was the Germans. Hitler had just declared war on Russia and Pavel's village was right near to the border. They escaped and somehow made their way down into Italy and finished up in Ashurst. He worked at the Prince of Wales until it closed and then he came here. I think he married a girl from Nook End." Then he walked over to his cupboard, took out a similar looking piece of metal that Pavel had just given him, and said: "Come on, I'll show you something you'll never see the like of again."

They walked along a dimly lit corridor to the old Copper Rolling Mill. It was like something out of Dante's Inferno.

"We're stopping production here next week. The new mill will be able to handle all this on the night shift. It's the end of an era for this place."

It was hot and smoky. They could see Pavel stood by the rollers in the middle of the room. As the copper bar came out of the first pair of rollers, it was Pavel's job to take hold of the near molten strip which was about an inch wide, swivel it round and feed it into the next pair of rollers. They were not turning as fast so the copper strip spilled out on the floor, like an angry snake, hissing and spitting sparks and smoke.

At the opposite side of the rollers stood the second handler. As the copper strip came out of that roller, again just like Pavel he had to catch hold of it with his grips, something like a very long pair of pliers, swivel it round and feed it into the third pair of rollers. Others did the same on the adjacent rollers, so that by the time the strip came out of the final roller it was about a quarter of an inch in diameter. Then it ran

76

down a long chute where it was sprayed and coiled up on to a drum.

"They make it look easy, but its very dangerous. The new mill will do this all automatically. It won't be as spectacular, but a lot safer."

It was turned eleven by this time. Billy took them up the stairs to level twenty four and unlocked the cubicle. It had been warm in his office. Here it was hot, but once the cubicle door was open they were able to shelter behind it while they looked inside. They could see the blizzard outside through the windows alongside the rectifier unit. Talk about going from one extreme to the other. At dinner time, one of Billy's men went out for pies; there were innumerable places they could be warmed up. They stayed there until half past three, by which time they had had enough.

They went back down to the office, but Billy had finished his shift at two o clock. His replacement, Jimmy Creevy, asked them what they had been doing and would they be coming back. The talk moved on to the weather. It was still pretty bad. In fact, one of the labourers had gone missing. No one quite knew where he was. Just before twelve o clock he said he was nipping home for his dinner as he normally did and one of the handlers asked him to call in his house for some clean socks, but no more had been seen or heard of him. The weather was bad, but surely not that bad.

Alan and Yorky walked back to the drawing office, pleased with their day and still feeling the heat from the furnace in their bones. As they walked through the Mechanical section, it was strangely quiet and not a soul about. And on Yorky's board they could see a large sheet of white paper on which one of the others had written:

WE WERE ALL SENT HOME AT THREE WITH PAY.
LANCASHIRE SIX YORKSHIRE ONE.

14
"I REALLY LIKE YOU"

January 1963 was just one long struggle against the elements. It was a struggle to get into work in the mornings. Sometimes the buses ran, sometimes they didn't. It was a struggle to keep warm once you had arrived at work. Most of the time the heating system worked but not all the time. And at the end of the day it was another struggle to get home.

Yorky and Alan made frequent trips to the Rolling Mill. It was a good number while it lasted, and they milked it for all it was worth. They enjoyed spending time with Billy. And they also got to know his chargehand, Mick Ellison.

Mick was one of the been everywhere, done everything, seen everybody brigade. If you had done it, then Mick had already done it quicker, longer or better. He was a likeable bloke but to put it bluntly, he told lies. To put it another way, his concept of reality was a combination of what he saw around him and what went on in his head. There was always an element of truth in his stories, but not much. Over the years he had acquired various nick names, Mad Mick, Fantasy Man and Kilroy being the most common. On the other hand, he was a real grafter whenever the occasion demanded it. When there was not much required of him, it was then that his mind would begin to wander and he would move off into his own little dream world. But he was good company, particularly when he started doing his imitations of Eddie Waring.

On their second visit, Alan asked Billy what had happened to the labourer Keith who had gone missing in the blizzard.

"Well you've never heard anything so daft," explained Billy. "He spent the afternoon in Colin's kitchen. You remember, I told you that Colin had asked him to call at his house and get him some clean socks. He lent him his front door key just in case his wife was out. Well she was, so Keith went straight in. Colin's dog was there but it never even barked when it saw Keith. It knew him well, Keith had been to the house many times, he only lives in the next street. But of course that had been when either Colin or Joyce had been there.

"He found the socks on the maiden in the kitchen, where Colin had told him, but when he tries to leave, Sasha won't let him out. It snaps at Keith each time he makes a move towards the door. Joyce had nipped out to her mother's, but she never came back until after five. As soon as she walked into the house, Sasha went back to being a big softy. Keith couldn't believe he had spent all afternoon there and lost four hours pay for it."

Except for Mick, who had started a job in the Foundry, the rest of the Drawing Office just had to grin and bear it. There was little they could do, except wear extra clothes, engage in physical jerks every hour or so and top up their morning drink with a drop of whisky.

One person who was not that affected by the Artic conditions sweeping across the north of England was Thelma. Each morning she would get up around ten and come down to a warm kitchen and a hot breakfast. Then she would spend the rest of the morning talking with Granny and listening to Grandad.

He would talk for hours about his childhood, his school days and his time spent down the pit. He would tell her about all the relatives, where they lived and what they did. He talked about the war, being captured and working down the lead mine. He told her about the death of Queen Victoria and how they had celebrated the coronation of Edward the Seventh. He just went on and on. Thelma was fascinated by it all, she had never heard anything like it. Granny had. She had heard it all before, many times, but she never ceased to enjoy hearing him talk.

Most of Granny's tales centred around the house they were sat in, the house where she had been born Mary Isabella Tabern on 28th of March 1891. She spoke at length of her own mother, who after giving birth to six children had died when Granny was thirteen. She told Thelma what it was like during the war, not knowing for months if Grandad was alive or dead, and the strange sensation she felt on hearing he had been taken prisoner. And she also talked of holidays they had enjoyed and the time they had taken Alan to Hoylake on the Wirral and he had cried when he saw the tide coming in.

The more they talked, the more questions Thelma would ask: "When was the house built? When did you first have a wireless? How did you know when Grandad was coming home after the War? What did he do in the General Strike? How much did things cost? How much did he get paid?" She never stopped, she was so interested in everything about the place and its past.

"Ee, you are just like Alan, always wanting to know, always asking questions," Granny would say lovingly to her.

In this way Thelma began to build up a picture of life in Ashurst, stretching back nearly eighty years. She began to develop a deep knowledge of the Holding and the Tabern family tree. And as she asked questions of different relatives, photographs were produced to put faces to names. At the same time comparisons were made between different people. "Do you not think Stanley looks like our Albert?" or "Alan's got our Eric's frown on this one, hasn't he?" Granny would say.

In the afternoon, if the weather was not too bad, Grandad would call on various relatives to make sure they were alright. During the course of each week he would visit "our Doris", his sister, and "your Doris", Granny's sister. He would walk up to Canal Street where Granny's eldest brother Herbert and his wife May lived. They rarely went out of their house since both were quite poorly. On the way back he would call in to see old Bob, his friend of over sixty years, and who now lived sadly on his own. While he was away, the kitchen would be transformed into a classroom.

One afternoon Granny had been making a cake. She noticed how keenly Thelma was watching her every move. "Would you like to have a go, love?" she asked. Thelma's eyes lit up as she nodded keenly. Granny soon found she had a very willing apprentice. It was amazing how quickly her young lodger picked things up. Within a few weeks she had grasped the basics and under Granny's close supervision was making their evening meal. One evening Alan had eaten a couple of scones and then said, "Up to your usual high standard, eh Granny." He didn't know at that stage that Thelma had made them. It was praise indeed for her. She would not have been able to do that less than a month before.

But as she began to get better, Thelma began to think about the future. She knew she would soon be well enough to go back to work. Would that mean she would have to leave Silkstone Street? Compared to where she was now staying, ten Grasmere Avenue was a cold draughty house where the food was stodgy and where every evening Auntie Lil watched the most trashy programmes on the television. And worse than that she would often sleep through them, snoring loudly as she did, hardly the best environment for Thelma and her library books.

But she was grateful to Auntie Lil. If it hadn't been for her, Thelma would have had nowhere to live. But after a few weeks living where she had felt so much at home, the thought of leaving saddened her. She knew she would have to raise the matter soon. Who would it be best to talk to first? Granny or Alan, or maybe Alan's Mum. But before she could make up her mind, it was all decided for her.

Alan had called round one Saturday afternoon. No football or rugby was being played in Lancashire again. The ground was too hard and there was still mountains of snow about, but at least the sun was shining.

"Why don't you take Thelma into the park," said Granny, "I don't think she's been outside the house this year." It was true. Her coat hadn't moved from under the stairs where it had been put on Christmas Day. Walking across the park was the first time that they had been on their own together since Christmas Eve. Whenever he had seen her since then, Granny or Grandad or one or other of the relatives had always been in the same room or within hearing range. Now they had an opportunity to talk more freely, and of course he had something to tell her.

80

Alan never thought things would turn out like they had when he had seen her on that bus on Christmas Eve. He had been out with other girls but had never met any of their parents before. Once that starts you never know where it might end up. With Thelma it was the other way round. She had become part of the family and, except for being in Mario's coffee bar with her, he had never been out with her.

She was clinging to his arm for support. She still felt weak and there was still this worry about where she was going to live. Finally she could stand it no longer. Now was the time to find out. She looked up at him, her face half hidden between one of Grandad's woollen scarves and her funny little woolly hat.

"Alan, what's going to happen to me? Has your Granny had enough of me. Have I stayed too long? I don't want to take anything for granted. Should I offer to leave now that I'm getting better? Granny has been so good to me, and your Grandad. I'll always be grateful. I'll never forget what they have done but if I've got to go I'll understand. What should I do?"

It was always the same when she was worried or upset. Her words would come flooding out in a torrent, the phrases she used not always directly connected. When something was wrong, her face would show it. As Alan looked at her, out of the corner of his eye to his dismay he saw one of the moulders from the foundry exercising his dog. He turned Thelma sharply and began walking her in the opposite direction. At this very moment in time, the last person in the world he wanted to talk to was Roy Ferris with his endless complaints about Ashurst Council.

"Listen, Thelma. We all know just how much you like being at Granny's and how much you appreciate what they have done for you. But don't forget it has been good for them as well. They both enjoy having you there. Whenever my mum sees Granny, you are the main thing she talks about. She's been great to us all, but somehow it has been different with you."

"How do you mean?" asked Thelma, clinging closely to his arm and savouring every moment of their close contact.

"My mum thinks it is partly because she sees her great grandmother in you. You see, both her grandmothers died before Granny was born but great grandmother Tabern lived until Granny was about eight. It would appear that Granny spent a lot of time with her when she was small."

"But what's the link between her and me?"

"It must be your accent that has triggered things off in Granny's head. You see, Granma Tabern also came from Wales, and just like you she had no family."

"How did she come to live in Ashurst?"

"Granny's great grandfather, Billy Tabern the watchmaker, met her in Southport. She was a domestic servant in a big hotel, a bit like you were. It must have been love

81

at first sight. They were married within a year."

Then he went on, "Granny has got a real soft spot for you Thelma. She thinks you are a smashing kid."

He paused for a moment and then said, "And so do I."

It was the first time he had said anything like that to her. Of course, by everything he had done since Christmas Eve, he had shown what he thought about her but this was the first time he had used words. They walked along silently for a few yards. She had come to realise that he did not find it easy to express his feelings, but it was much better that way than the cheap talk you get from some people. "And so do I" had obviously come from the heart. It was only four words and yet it conveyed so much to her.

A man who seemed familiar walked past. He nodded to Alan and smiled at her. She was glad he didn't speak, she was still hearing the echo of those words "And so do I" in her head. They carried on walking until Alan broke the silence.

"Are you alright, Thelma? You've gone all quiet. Is something wrong?"

"No, Alan. Not at all. It was the last thing you said that made me feel so good."

"You mean when I said Granny had a soft spot for you and thought you were a smashing kid."

"And the rest Alan, you also said...."

"And so do I, well I do, I really like you."

He stopped walking and turned his face towards her. She looked up at him, sensing his next move and knowing how willingly she would respond. They were quite oblivious to their surroundings. He was not bothered that some of the neighbours might also be in the park. Slowly, their faces moved towards each other. He could feel her warm breath on his chin as he looked straight into her eyes. Thelma hoped that this was going to be the start of something new between them. Was he now going to act a little less like her big brother and a bit more like her boyfriend. Surely it could now be said she was going out with him. Slowly their faces moved closer and at the very moment their lips were about to make contact, they were interrupted by barking and the gruff voice of Roy Ferris.

"Here boy, here boy, good dog. Hello Greeno," and witin minutes, as Alan knew he would, he began talking about the next major event to affect the whole country's economy, the decision by Ashurst Council to stop running the trolley buses.

It was lucky for them that it started to snow again. It gave them a good excuse to get away from him. Roy was alright in his place, the trouble was it hadn't been dug yet. They walked back to the house arm in arm. The wind had got up again and was blowing the snow in their faces making any conversation almost impossible. Thelma still did not know whether or when she would have to leave. But it didn't matter as much now. Alan had said what she wanted to hear, "I really like you".

When they walked into the house, his young nephew was playing stonies in the hall. As they closed the front door, Granny called out from the kitchen.

"Who is it, Michael?"

"It's only Uncle Alan and Auntie Thelma," he replied.

Michael and his dad stayed for an hour and as they were leaving Mrs. Kilshaw called. By the time they had all gone it was nearly six. As they sat down for their meal, Thelma was feeling exhausted but happy. So much had happened since the last time she had been outside. The main thing was of course with Alan. She recalled the first time she had seen him. It was in the Print room one morning in July. 'I Can't Stop Loving You' by Ray Charles had just risen to the top of the Hit Parade. After that, whenever she saw him at work he would always stop for a chat. He seemed a really nice lad, and sometimes she felt sorry for him when she heard the others having a go at him. As time went on she began to grow very fond of him.

After a while she heard he was off work from an injury playing football. This might be her opportunity. If they sent a get well card round she would write 'Love From Thelma' on it. That would get some tongues wagging she hoped. But no one did, or if they did, it never came into the Planning Office. By the time she saw him again, Frank Ifield was at the top of the Hit Parade with 'Lovesick Blues', and that was what Thelma now had. But nothing further happened until she was sat on that bus outside the Co-op Hall on Christmas Eve, with the prospects of a lonely few days in front of her. And then everything in her life had changed.

Granny brought in the meal, a shepherd's pie she had made while they were in the park. As she put the plates before them, she said, as she always did, "Be careful the plate's mad hot." They were, and so was the food. The piccalli and the beetroot went round the table and, just as they were about to start, Grandad uttered a few words that completely shattered Thelma's mood of contentment

"So you're leaving us tomorrow then, are you, love?" he said with a smile on his face.

She was taken completely by suprise. It was the last thing she expected. She couldn't believe her ears. She couldn't believe that Alan hadn't mentioned anything about it to her in the park. She began to wish she had raised the matter earlier. If she had asked Granny whether she wanted her to leave now that she was getting better, Granny would have almost certainly said not yet. And surely when she had to go they would give her a few days notice, time to get used to the idea, unappealing as it was.

Her whole body went numb. She no longer felt hungry. Perhaps they had had enough of her. They were both in their seventies. Maybe it was just too much for them to have a lodger in the house any longer. Would she be invited to visit them after she had left. Once a week maybe, or perhaps just now and again. But no matter what happened she would always remember them with such gratitude. They had taken her in, a complete stranger, and looked after her and made her so welcome. She would never forget Christmas 1962. Despite being so ill, it was still the best one she had ever had.

She could not think how to reply. She looked at Granny, but she had turned towards Alan. Was she embarrassed about it? Was it all going to end on a sour note?

"Have you not told Thelma?" Granny said "I bet you forgot. I bet it went right out of your head."

"I'm sorry Thelma, I would have told you when we were in the park, but what with Roy and his daft dog and then it starting to snow, I forgot."

So Alan did know. How long had he known and said nothing. It should have been the first thing he said to her. She would have accepted it a lot more easily from him, particularly now that he had told her what he felt about her.

She looked closely at him as he carried on speaking, waiting for the details of her departure from Silkstone Street.

"You're invited up to our house tomorrow. My mum says you can come for your dinner. You'll be more than welcome, you can stay for your tea and your supper too if you want to."

Thelma uttered an enormous sigh of relief. She ought to have known they wouldn't have asked her to leave at such short notice. She was annoyed with herself for even thinking badly of them. It was just Grandad's smile when he had spoken that had upset her. Now she realised it was only because he thought Alan had told her when he hadn't.

"I don't think she should stay out so late, Alan. It will be the first time she's been out proper!"

"I was only repeating the exact words you used when I asked if Thelma could come for her dinner on Christmas Day."

"How can you remember so clearly something that was said over a month ago, and forget what your mum said yesterday?" mused Grandad. "Poor Thelma must have had a real shock when I said that. She must have thought we were going to throw her out on to the street. You're a real dreamer Alan, somebody will have to knock some sense into that thick head of yours one day."

Then, turning to Thelma and shaking her head, Granny said, "He's always been the same. Ee, I could tell you some tales about him."

"Like the time he nearly burned the house down," smiled Grandad.

Thelma suddenly felt a lot better. Her appetite returned as quickly as she had lost it, but she wanted to keep any discussion about her leaving until a more appropriate time so she quickly asked Granny what he had done.

"He was six, I think. Their Joan had brought him down one Saturday and then gone off into town. I had just laid a fire in the front room. I lit it and as the sticks began to catch, I put a large sheet of newspaper and a shovel in front of it, so that it would draw better. Just keep your eyes on this Alan, I said, while I go and get some coal. When I came back the paper was all ablaze. I thought I told you to watch the fire, I said to him. Yes, I am, it's great isn't it. Heavens knows whatever would have happened if it had fallen on the carpet!"

The rest of the meal was spent with Granny and Grandad talking about Alan's follies over the years. He even added a few tales from work, ones they had not heard before. It would have probably gone on longer if they had not been interrupted by Uncle Stanley and his daughter Marion calling round to see what time to pick Thelma up in the morning.

After tea they watched television for a while, but by nine o' clock Granny was shooing her off to bed. She was more than happy to go, tired from that little walk in the snow. And as she lay tucked up and warm, listening to the blizzard outside, and with Little Ted in her arms, she thought how much better life had become since Christmas Eve. She felt so good at what Alan had said in the park. She felt so pleased that she had been invited out for her dinner tomorrow and how good Uncle Stanley was giving up his time to take her there and probably bring her back as well.

But most of all, she thought how lucky she was to be looked after by someone else's Granny in the way she was. The home and the soap works in Cardiff, the holiday camp in Rhyl, that hotel in Liverpool, all seemed so far away, even Grasmere Avenue. And as she lay there she also wondered what would she be doing now if she had caught an earlier bus on Christmas Eve. But that was something she would never know.

15
THELMA'S STORY

It was a bright sunny morning. There was not a cloud in the sky and the snow was sparkling in the sun. Grandad was in the yard chopping sticks; Granny had nipped across the street to see Mrs Higham. Thelma was sat in the kitchen in front of the fire. She loved to sit there, pick a large piece of coal from the scuttle, place it right in the centre of the fire and watch it burn. With a little imagination she could see all sorts of faces. It was such a relaxing way to pass the time.

After a while Granny returned. "Make us a cup of tea while I get warm, will you love?" she said as she took off her coat, and playfully pinched Thelma's last piece of toast. "Are you all ready for your day out?" But before Thelma could say anything she went on, "You know that little diary you got at Christmas, have you put anything in it yet?".

"No, I haven't, it's still upstairs. Why?"

"Will you make a note in it for next Thursday. Mrs. Higham has invited us to tea. She would like to meet you. She's heard all about you."

The invitation did not come as a complete surprise to Thelma. She had half expected something like this soon. She had already met Mrs McGinty, Mrs Kilshaw and Mrs Pilkington from next door. In many ways they were all like Granny. The way they talked and what they talked about, the way they dressed and what they did during the course of each week. They were all a product of the same environment, a northern industrial town dominated by the work that took place there.

As they were talking, Uncle Stanley walked in wearing his overalls.

"Don't tell me you are working today, Stanley?"

"We're putting a new boiler in the Town Hall kitchen. The old one has been leaking for ages."

"Have you time for a bite to eat?"

"Aye, go on then."

Two fried eggs, three pieces of bacon, two rounds of toast and a mug of tea later, he decided they had better get going.

As his van pulled up outside the house, Alan's Mum came out to meet them. After a few words with her brother, she took Thelma's arm and led her into the house. As they stepped into the kitchen she called out, "Alan, put your toys away now, your

86

visitor has arrived." Then she took Thelma's coat, woolly hat and Grandad's scarf and ushered her into the living room where her son was sat reading the Reynolds News.

"Dinner will be in about twenty minutes, and before you say anything young lady, no I don't want any help. And if I do I've got this big strapping lad to do it for me. So you just sit down and take it easy."

Sunday dinner had always been pretty much the same at thirty two Chisnall Avenue; roast lamb, roast potatoes, mashed carrots sometimes with peas or cauliflower and eaten while listening to Family Favourites and the Billy Cotton Band Show. But today the radio was silent and there was a large bottle on the table.

"Would you like a drink Thelma? It's a special wine, West Lancashire Mosel."

"Yes, please, but I didn't know grapes grew up here."

"They grow on a small stretch of coast just north of Southport. It gets washed by the Gulf Stream in June. It's a freak of nature, an oceanic oddity the experts call it."

Thelma tasted it. She didn't know anything about wine and this was nothing special, but perhaps it was an acquired taste. She put down her glass and said it was quite nice. She saw his mum smiling and then Alan burst out laughing.

"It's corporation pop," and when he saw she didn't know what he meant, he went on, "it's water, tap water with a spoonful of sugar in it."

"Don't you worry," said his mum seeing the look on Thelma's face, "You won't be the first person he's pulled that one on."

She was easily persuaded to have a second helping of dinner and this was followed by a large plateful of apple pie and custard. When they had finished his mum said to her son:

"You can side the table and wash up. We're going to sit back and put our feet up".

At this, Thelma began to wonder whether to bring up the whole business of continuing to stay at Granny's, but it was not to be.

"I know that you like looking at the family photographs. Do you want to see ours?" And with that his mum brought out a large cardboard box from the sideboard and sat down beside her.

As Alan was washing up, he had a brief visit from one of his friends. When he went back into the living room a few minutes later, his mum asked: "Was that Geoff Platt? What did he want?"

"He wants me to help him re-wire his granma's house. She's had a flood."

"Red Martha, you always liked her, didn't you?"

"I do. She's a smashing old lady."

Turning to Thelma, she said, "If ever there's a revolution in Ashurst, Martha Turner will be right at the front of it with a big red flag. It's her that Alan's got half of his funny ideas from, isn't it?"

"You have to admit that a lot of what she's said over the years has come true."

"I know that. Listen, I like her. I voted for her when she stood for the Council. It's just I don't agree with everything she's done. Everything is either black or white with her. But listen we're not going to fall out over politics today."

The reference to Red Martha intrigued Thelma. She had first heard about her after a CND meeting when they had gone for a drink with a few older campaigners who had come down from Manchester. From what she had heard, Geoff Platt's grandmother had certainly been a real firebrand in the past, although none of the Young Socialists seemed to have a good word for her.

"Alan, do you remember that year we went to Rhyl with Auntie Kitty and Uncle Billy, that time our Paul fell off that donkey? Did you know that Thelma used to work there?"

It suddenly struck him he knew so little about her. It had come as a shock when she had told him that she had been brought up in a home. He had always assumed she had a family somewhere, and suprising as it was he had never had a chance to ask about her past all the time she had been living at Granny's.

"You hardly know a thing about me, do you? None of you. I must still be a complete mystery to you all."

"It's not that we aren't interested, Thelma," explained his mum. "We were sure you would tell us about yourself when you were ready, you know when you were better. After all you have been very poorly."

"Well now that I'm getting better, perhaps I ought to tell you. It's not that bad, I'm not an alien from Mars."

They both sat quietly as she continued.

"I was born in a place called Tonyrefail near Pontypridd. When I was a baby my mum died. She musn't have had any close relatives so I was put in an orphanage in Cardiff. I lived there until I was sixteen. Then I got a job in a soap works nearby. I didn't like it, or the hostel I had moved into. So in the summer I went to work in a holiday camp in Rhyl with three other girls. I liked it there, but at the end of the season they sacked us all. That was where I met Beryl. She had gone to work there because she wanted to get away from her dad. She got us both fixed up working in a hotel in Liverpool. It was near enough for her to visit her mum easily. But after a few weeks she fell ill and had to go home. I stayed on, I didn't really have any choice. I had nowhere else to go. The place was a bit rough to say the least, but I liked Liverpool.

I used to go and see Beryl every other week, and when she got better we began to plan what we were going to do in the summer. Then there was a fire in the hotel and I got finished. The only person I could turn to was Beryl. She had fallen out with her dad again and was living with her auntie in Grasmere Avenue. When they heard what had happened, she said I could live with them. So that's how I came to live in Ashurst. I got a job in Woolworths, and me and Beryl started to save up and make plans for the summer. At the time she was going out with a lad from Gillarsfield. He was quite nice, but Beryl had set her heart on going to London, but then she found out she was going to have a baby. So instead they got married and went to live at Nook End. Luckily her auntie said I could carry on living with her."

"Well, you have had a hard time of it."

She just smiled sadly.

"And how much do you know about being born in, where was it, Tony, what was it?"

"Tonyrefail. It was only a couple of months before I left the home. We had a new person in charge. She was really nice. Not like the old battle-axe we'd had all the time before her. A few weeks after she'd arrived she had a big clear out in the attic and found an envelope addressed to my mum at nine Rosemount Terrace, Tonyrefail.

"So the following Saturday I went there on the bus. It would be a nice ride out if nothing else, I thought. It was a terraced street, but no number nine. I asked next door and this lady told me they had bought it and knocked through to make it a larger house. When I told them why I had come, she invited me in and brought down a suitcase they had found in the loft.

"I couldn't believe my luck. In it were some clothes, some photographs, and a few letters. We had a cup of tea and then her husband took me round to see the daughter of the couple he had bought the house from. She actually remembered me being there. Sadly her parents had died, but she promised to ask around to see if anybody could remember anything about me. When we got back to the house his wife made a meal for us. They were really nice and invited me to go back there any time. I remember how strange it was seeing a picture of your mum for the first time. I kept looking at it all the way back to Cardiff on the bus".

She paused for breath and looked at Alan's Mum. She had tears in her eyes.

"Oh, you poor child, you poor child," she said and leaned forward, took Thelma in her arms and hugged her. They remained locked together for what seemed an age, then Thelma broke free and said.

"Never mind, that was all in the past. Do you want to know how I got the job at Wilkinson's?"

His mum sat back looking into Thelma's face. Then she leaned forward and hugged her again. "You poor child, you poor child". With her hand Thelma waved Alan away and mouthed the words "cup of tea". By the time he had returned, they were both sat together quietly. Thelma's brief account of her life had really upset Alan's mum.

"Just a minute, I'll go and swill my face," she said, and as she went upstairs he sat down besides her."You poor kid, I didn't know." He took her in his arms and kissed her. He ran his hand over her face and looked closely in her eyes. All this time he had known her and he hardly knew a thing about her.

They were still locked together as his mum came down the stairs. She indicated they should both remain on the sofa.

"Sorry about that. So how did you come to work at Wilkinson's, Thelma?"

"It was after I had been living with Auntie Lil a few weeks. One night she had a visitor. As soon as he opened his mouth I could tell he came from South Wales. He was really nice. He asked me how long I had been living in Ashurst and where I worked. When I told him what I was doing he asked me if I would like a job at Wilkinson's. I hadn't a clue what they did there. Is your hand writing good, are you neat and tidy and good with figures, he asked. The outcome of it was I went for an interview and started there a week later."

"It must have been Charlie Spencer. You dropped on there."

"Yes, it was."

"I bet it was a lot better working there than in Woolworths," said his mum. "What was your first day like?"

"It was chaotic. The Work Study were re-organising their filing system. We were so busy. It all had to be done in two weeks. I even worked overtime, but they managed it in the end. The next day the boss Mr Butterworth called us all into his office and thanked us. And then Bill Riley stood up and said they all ought to give a special thanks to the new girl as it wouldn't have gone half as smoothly if she hadn't done her bit. They all clapped and I felt embarrassed. After that Mr. Butterworth told me things wouldn't be quite so hectic and that part of my job would be getting drawings from the Print Room for the planners.

"Is that when you got to know me laddo?" asked his mum, now back to her usual self. "When did you first set eyes on him?"

"Tony Cropper took me into the Print Room and introduced me to Big Joan and Rita. There were three or four draughtsmen in there at the time and Joan said, 'No more swearing in here you lads, we've got a lady with us now', and then Alan popped up from behind one of the cabinets and said that she'd be the first one they had had in there for a long time.

"That would be around the time he was on his crusade against British Railways. I bet the next thing he did was to ask you to sign his petition."

"Yes, he did and he was so suprised when I told him I had already signed it. Somebody had already been to our house. I remember, we couldn't get rid of him. He kept telling us about the time he had fought in the Spanish Civil War."

90

"So you took a shine to him right from the start did you. I bet he never even noticed."

"I don't think he did, but I used to live in hope every day he would ask me out. That's why I spent so much time in the Print Room."

"Didn't you see that she had a twinkle in her eye for you"

He hadn't. Around that time he had been going out with a nurse from Knotty Ash. But there was not that much special about her, and what with the distance and her crazy shift system it slowly petered out.

Then his Mum asked what had happened on Christmas Eve, how had it all started. To Thelma it all seemed such a long time ago, but actually it was only six weeks, such a short time in which her whole life had been transformed.

"I'd been to see Beryl and their baby. I'd bought it a little present. I came back into town on the bus. I must have waited over half an hour for it. When it stopped outside the Co-op Hall I saw him waving to me. I was off like a shot."

"Was he drunk? Was he trying to imitate Marlon Brando, like he usually does when he has had a few?"

"I don't think so. All I can remember was that I was frozen and he was stood there with his mac over his shoulder and his jacket undone just wearing his shirt."

"So you went off to Marios, did you?"

"Yes. And when he invited me to spend Christmas Day with his family, I couldn't believe my good luck."

"You didn't want to come at first, did you? You said it'd be too much work for my mum and she wouldn't be expecting you and all the rest of it?"

"Alan, there was nothing more I wanted to do than come. I didn't want to be on my own all over Christmas. But I was terrified at the thought of walking into a room full of people I didn't know and sitting round the table with them."

"Well, you were very brave, love. I don't think I could have done that."

"It was a good job we were the first to arrive, and of course Granny was so good to me right from the start."

"Well, we're all glad you did come. We'll never forget that Christmas Day, will we?"

Before she could say any more, they heard the back door being opened, and then into the room burst Michael and Peter followed by Alan's brother Paul and his wife Dorothy.

"Hello Granma, hello Uncle Alan, hello Auntie Thelma," the boys both said with the younger one demanding a kiss from the three of them.

"Hello Thelma," said Dorothy, "how nice to see you. You're looking a lot better. How are you?" Before Thelma could reply Peter was climbing onto her knee and Michael was pulling at her frock and asking her would she play Ludo with them.

91

The next hour was spent with Dorothy, Paul and his mum chatting away in the living room while Alan, Thelma and the two boys played in the front room. While they were in there Paul commented about the noise Thelma was making.

"She's like a big kid. She's as bad as our Michael."

His mum looked at him sternly and said:

"Paul, she told us about herself just before you arrived and where she was brought up. It brought tears to my eyes. Perhaps she's just making up for a childhood she never had. She's a smashing kid, I won't hear a word against her. Let her enjoy herself. She can make as much racket as she wants to in this house."

"I'm sorry mum, I wasn't being nasty. All I said was she's a bit noisy. Anyway, we're going to take the pair of them out next Sunday. The boys are going to their Auntie Val's so we thought we'd have a run out to Ainsdale. A few hours on the beach would do her a world of good."

And it certainly did. There was still snow on the ground but the sun was shining brightly. They drove down the East Lancs Road as far as Windle Island, up the Rainford by-pass and across the flat West Lancashire countryside to the coast.

It was almost mid-day when they got out of the car. The sun was quite strong, although they still had to walk briskly to keep warm. Alan had been there before, but he had never seen it so deserted. Suddenly, out of nowhere a little dog appeared snapping at their ankles. "Don't say Roy Ferris has come, as well," he laughed, but it was an old man with a walking stick who finally appeared and chatted to them for a few minutes.

Clouds appeared in the sky and the temperature began to fall. They ate their sandwiches and on the way back called in to see Dorothy's sister who lived at Clinkham Wood on the outskirts of St.Helens. By the time they arrived back at Chisnall Avenue they were starving.

As they walked into the house it was almost three o clock. "That's good timing. Dinner will be ready in ten minutes," and then Alan's mum went on, "By gum, you've all caught the sun, haven't you, and look at your face Thelma, it's brought your freckles out as well." And with that she gave her a little hug and commented: "You're looking a lot better than when I first met you."

"Did I look poorly then?"

"You did love. You looked pale and drawn. I remember thinking to myself, this girl needs fattening up a bit, and look at you now, old chubby chops."

Thelma took her coat off and looked in the mirror. It was true what his mum had said. Her face was much fuller, her skin had plenty of colour to it, and her freckles covered her face again. Once she used to wish she didn't have them, but now it didn't bother her at all. The people she had got to know over the last few weeks wouldn't suddenly stop liking her just because she had a few kisses from the sun on her face. In fact, she now knew how much all his family liked her and how much she liked them. And she knew how much she loved two, no three, of them in particular.

They demolished the meal. The four of them were ravenous. They sat down and chatted for a while and then Paul and Dorothy left taking Thelma with them. It was only a ten minute drive back to Silkstone Street, but by the time they pulled up outside the house their passenger was fast asleep.

16
THE PIT BROW LASSES

"Well, if you are going back to work Thelma..." but before Granny could say any more there was a knock on the front door. She put down her cup and went to answer it. While she was away, Thelma began to wonder how the sentence would end. Perhaps Granny was going to ask her if she would now like to go back to Grasmere Avenue. Well she wouldn't, but obviously she would go if she had to.

She had just returned from the doctors with the news that she would be ready for work in a couple of weeks time. She had been living at Silkstone Street for almost two months. When Doctor Jackson had first seen her, he had considered sending her to the hospital, but in the end it was Granny who had nursed her back to health. It must have been hard work for her, traipsing up and down the stairs in that first week, and for Grandad too, but she had never heard them complain once.

But now she was going to be alright maybe they just wanted to be on their own again. They had not had an easy life. They deserved a rest in their old age and particularly after what they had done for her since Christmas, but she would be so sorry to leave. She had loved living with them in their big terraced house with all its old fashioned furniture.

"It was Mrs. Dean. She wouldn't come in. She never will."

She warmed her hands in front of the fire and went on, "As I was saying Thelma, now that you are going back to work,I think you'll need to get a new coat. That one you've got is no good for this sort of weather."

Thelma knew that only too well. It was only a summer coat. No wonder she never felt warm in it.

"And don't worry about the money. Grandad and me will buy it for you. We don't want you catching pneumonia again, do we."

Before she could say much more than thank you, Granny went on to say there was another thing too. Thelma's heart missed a beat. Was this a case of good news and bad news; a present to soften the blow of having to leave the best place that she had ever lived. Granny walked to the kitchen table and opened the drawer.

"What is it?"

"It's your front door key. You can come and go as you please now."

"You mean I can stay on."

"You've not been thinking I was going to ask you to leave when you got better, have you? Heaven forbid. I never thought. Of course you can stay. You can stay as long as you want. I wouldn't have it any other way."

Thelma threw her arms around her and hugged her.

"Oh Granny, you've been so good to me. I'm so lucky. I love living here and I don't know how I would have managed without you."

"I know you do, love. I know. But it's no more than you deserve. It was the least we could do for you. And after what I heard from our Doreen yesterday, I'm so glad we did."

"Why, what did she say?"

"What you had told her on Sunday, about seeing that picture of your mum for the first time and looking at it on the bus."

"It upset her, didn't it?"

"It did. And it upset me when you said you'd never been to a family dinner on Christmas Day before. I shed a few tears for you that night, I don't mind telling you."

"I know. I remember saying it. I felt awful. I thought I'd gone and spoiled everything."

"Well, it looks as though the very opposite has happened, doesn't it?"

Sat in that kitchen in front of the fire talking with Granny she felt so warm and safe. Thelma remembered the first time they had met and she had wrongly called her Mrs. Greenall. "Just call me Granny" she had replied and now Thelma did it almost as though she was her real grandmother. It somehow seemed so natural. And she remembered again being so ill and this lady who she hardly knew caring for her and nursing her back to health.

They talked about the weather, going back to work, whether to go to Wigan or St. Helens to look at coats, and what to do about lunch. It was of course the day they had been invited to visit Mrs. Higham across the street.

By now Thelma was really looking forward to going. She had already met a couple of Granny's neighbours and she just loved listening to the way they talked and what they talked about. And going out would also have a new element to it. No matter where she went, she had a place to return to that really was home. She couldn't wait to go out so that she could use the key to come back in again.

Around two o clock they left Grandad mending his boots in the wash house and walked across the street. As soon as they walked into Mrs. Higham's living room, Thelma wondered whether the whole street had been invited as well. There was an enormous spread on the table and the smell of baking in the kitchen. Mrs. Higham brought in a cup of tea for each of them and then produced a small bottle of whisky.

"Would you like a drop to celebrate my birthday? I'm seventy five today." Then, turning to Thelma she said, "Come on love, get some food in you while it's still there. There won't be much left once Mrs. Leatherbarrow starts."

"Who else is coming?" asked Granny.

"Mrs. Leatherbarrow, Mrs. Unsworth and Mrs. Eckersley. Our Billy will be calling round tonight so we'd better save a bit for him. Ernest is coming on Saturday with the children."

"Is he still in Preston?"

"Yes. He's still working at Dick Kerrs. I think they call it English Electrical or something now. I don't know why they couldn't keep the old name."

She poured a little more whisky into their cups and then said, "So, you're Alan's young lady friend are you. Well he has done well for himself."

Thelma nodded and asked how long had she known him.

"Ever since he was a baby. Mary used to bring him over in that rusty old pram they used to have. He was a lovely little thing. Then she chuckled and said, "I'll tell you a little story about him. It still makes me laugh but don't tell him. He'll only be embarrassed." She picked up a sandwich, indicated to Thelma to have another and went on.

"He must have only been about five. I saw him banging on Mary's front door one day. He was crying and holding his backside. I went over and asked him what the matter was." She imitated a child's voice, "I've done a job in my pants" and then went on, "He was in a terrible state. So I brought him round here, stripped him, washed him and put him in the spare bed. But don't tell him I told you. Mind you he's been here enough times since, he's probably forgotten. He put that socket on the wall for me and that fancy switch. It was just before he hurt his leg. Ee he's been in some scrapes. You ask him how he got that cut on his head. Geoff Platt did it on Wallwork's tip. They've always been good friends. Do you want another sandwich love, or a piece of cake?"

She chatted on for a while and then Thelma asked, "Who are all the people in that photograph."

Granny laughed and said, "I didn't think it would take her long before she started asking questions. She's just like Alan, always wanting to know about the past. I bet she knows more about Ashurst than half the people who live here."

Mrs. Higham pointed, "Do you see this one? That's me, that's Mrs. Unsworth and that's Mrs. Eckersley." Then turning to Granny she reminisced, "Do you remember Hilda Brady, little Hilda from Marsden street? She died last week. Their Maurice told me," and silently she mouthed the word cancer.

"It's a photograph of us pit brow lasses at the old Alexandra pit, love. They took it in 1905. I think they had just had a revolution in Russia. Ee, we should have had a

96

revolution on that pit brow. By gum it was a hard life up there. That's where I lost my little finger." She held up her left hand and there was a stump where the little finger should have been.

She moved onto the next photograph." That's me and our Billy on a Whit Sunday walk. I must have been about twelve. I know I hadn't started work. And that's my late husband Tom in his uniform just before they went to France. That's him with his sister Agnes after it was all over. That's his other sister Florence at Blackpool and this little baby here is me with my mother." Then she walked back to the table, picked up a scone and said "Ee, you'll not be wanting to hear about all these folk. They're all dead and buried now. All gone to the land of nod. Well most of them. Just a few of us left."

Thelma said nothing. She could have asked questions about all of them but perhaps now wasn't the time,. She had taken an immediate liking to Mrs. Higham and now that she was living in Silkstone Street they were neighbours. Perhaps she could pop over and see her now and again, just like Granny seemed to do.

"What do you do at Wilkinson's? Have you got a nice office job? It's a good place. They seem to look after their workers there. Not like in our day. Have another sandwich or a scone. I put some rum in the mixture. It gives it that edge. Ee, we'll all be drunk by tea-time. Still it's not every day you reach seventy five. How are Michael and Peter doing. You should get Paul to bring them over again. Paul used to come here often enough. Joan never liked coming, did she. How's her baby?"

At this point more of Mrs Higham's visitors arrived, Mrs Unsworth and Mrs Eckersley. They hung their coats in the hall and came in to be introduced. Mrs Higham did the honours. "This is Thelma, she's Alan's young lady friend. She's been very ill and she's been staying with Mary." They both said how pleased they were to meet her and hoped she would soon get better.

"How is Alan? I've not seen him for ages."

"I have," said Mrs Eckersley. "I signed his petition. He came to our house with it. I'm suprised he hasn't been to your house. He did a very good job keeping the station open, and he got his name in the paper too. I've kept a copy of it at home. Is he still at Wilkinson's? Where do you work, love? Are you there as well?"

Thelma told them that she had been there since July.

"Don't you talk nice. Are you from Wales? I always love to hear the Welsh people speak, it's so sweet in your ears," opined Mrs Unsworth. "Can you understand us Lancashire folk yet? We must sound pretty broad to you."

Thelma smiled and Mrs. Unsworth went on: "My son lives in Wales, at Llandudno, do you know it?" But before she could reply, Mrs Eckersley butted in, "and what do all your family think about you living in Ashurst?"

Granny quickly came in to say that Thelma didn't have any family and her mother had died when she was a baby. Mrs. Eckersley's face immediately showed her sorrow and her embarassment, "Oh, I am sorry love, I didn't know. Well you can't know when you meet somebody new, can you. One thing is for sure, you'll be in good hands with Mrs Holding. I'm sure she's making you feel at home."

"Oh, she is. She's been as good as a grandmother to me. She must have had some practice at it."

They all laughed, a little self-consciously, and then realising the need to change the subject Thelma said, "I've been looking at that photograph on the wall. You've both changed a bit since then".

They all laughed and Granny repeated what she had said earlier to Mrs. Higham about Thelma's inquisitive nature.

"Well, you ask us what you want to know, love but I don't think we'll be able to tell you anything interesting. We were only pit brow lasses. I don't think we were very important."

"What was a pit brow lass? What did you actually do?"

"Well the best way I can describe it to you is like this. Just imagine a belt about two foot wide slowly carrying coal that comes out of the pit. Our job was to clean it and make sure there were no big lumps before it all went to the railway wagons below the end of the belt."

"What do you mean, clean the coal?"

"We had to get rid of all the muck that was stuck to it."

"How did you do that?"

"The hard way, love. We had to do it with our bare hands. We just pulled it off and dropped it on to the floor."

"It must have been bad on your hands. Didn't you have any special gloves?"

"No, we didn't have anything. Your nails kept breaking and your hands were always chapped and blistered. And there was no first aid. If you cut your hand, well you just had to wait until you got home."

"How many of you were there?"

"About a dozen on our belt, half on each side, all in one shed."

"It wasn't really a shed," explained Mrs Unsworth. "It had a roof and that, but the sides only came down to just below your shoulders. The wind would blow right through you sometimes, and if it was raining you'd get wringing wet if you were on the wrong side."

"Couldn't you move to get away from the rain?"

"Oh no, once you were put in your place for the day you had to stay there. Even if there was a hole in the roof and the rain was dripping on your head you had to stay put. I remember Freda Martlew, she's dead now, God bless her. She tried to move a couple of feet towards a drier spot. Old Sam Grundy, he wouldn't allow her to. When he wasn't looking she tried it again and do you know what he did? He nailed a wooden box to the floor and made her stand in it. He made our life a misery, he did. Yet every Sunday he would be in church, praising the Lord. I hope he rots in Hell."

"What time did you start? How long did you work every day?"

"We had to be there before the belt started moving at six. If you were late, well you couldn't even start. You just got sent home. Usually we worked until half three."

"Did you have a break or anything?"

"We had twenty minutes to eat our dinner. That would be two jam butties and a flask of cold tea. And another thing, you couldn't just stop and go to the lavvy when you wanted to. You were only allowed to go twice a day. No good if you had the runs. I've seen Old Sam send a young girl home because she had spent too long attending to the call of nature."

Then Mrs. Higham joined in. "You know Thelma, you weren't even allowed to talk. If Old Sam heard you and he was in a bad mood, he'd just point at you and grunt "thee, wom.""

"What does wom mean?"

"It's an old Lancashire word. It means home. It was just his way of telling you to skedaddle."

"You were always cold up there," chirped in Mrs. Eckersley, "especially round your feet. It was worse if it was raining when you left home in the morning. You'd be wet when you got to work and you'd be wet all day. There was no fancy cloakroom to hang your coat up in. And there was no heating either. I was glad when I got married and left. Five years of misery it was for me, five long years."

"Yes, it was bad," said Mrs. Unsworth, "but we had some good times up there as well."

"Good times, I don't know about that - I must have been on the lavvy when you had any good times."

"Couldn't you do anything about the way they treated you? Didn't you have a union?"

"We were in the union for a bit but they never did anything for the lasses. The men who ran it were never interested. They should have been but they weren't."

"They were pretty interested in us on a Saturday night, that's for sure. But once we got back to work on Monday, they had forgotten all their promises."

Thelma could sense that the three of them were keen to talk, so she went on asking questions.

"How much did you get paid when you first started?"

99

"Ee, I can't remember," said Mrs. Unsworth. "Whatever it was, it was nowhere near enough for what we did. I just gave it all to my mother and she gave me threepence spend for the week."

"I got seven and fourpence when I started," said Mrs. Eckersley. "I remember that because I used to give my mother the seven shillings and I kept the fourpence. But it was a bit easier for you. You could walk it there in ten minutes from where you lived. It took me over half an hour from our house."

"Where did you live then?"

"Behind the Hotties in Golbourne Street."

"Whatever were the Hotties?"

"It was a flash behind Elliott's chemical works, love. Oh, if you don't know what a flash is, it's a big pond, water in a hole caused by subsidence. Hot water used to pour into this flash from the works. It was beautiful to look at in the winter when there was snow on the banks and steam rising from the water. The lads used to swim in it in their bare nack. But they wouldn't go near when it had turned red. It was poisonous then. I remember one day a man who lived near us walked past with a dog. One of the lads threw a stick into the water and the dog jumped in to get it. Next time we saw the man he was on his own. I asked him where his dog was. 'At home sick. It's that bloody water, it's poisoned him,' he screamed. A few weeks later it died. It was a lovely little thing."

"Have they not filled it all in now?" asked Mrs. Higham.

"Aye, and not before time," said Mrs. Unsworth. They did it after they closed Elliott's down. Our Albert worked there when he was a lad. You wouldn't believe how bad some of that place was."

"Do you remember the Green House. That was the worst of the lot."

"Whatever was that, was it full of windows and glass?"

"Ee, no lass, it was called the Green House because your skin would start to turn green after you had been there a while. One of my friends went there straight from school, her two sisters worked there as well. They all died before they saw forty."

They carried on talking in this way. They were clearly enjoying telling Thelma about themselves. And as they talked, they continued to eat and drink. Soon the bottle of whisky was empty. Then Mrs. Higham put some food on a tray. "I'll just nip and see Mrs. McGinty. She would have liked to be here, but she can hardly walk now. Her legs are really bad." As she went out she said, "I'll leave the front door open. I wonder where Mrs. Leatherbarrow has got to?"

By the time she returned, they were all getting ready to leave. "Five past five and we're still alive," said Mrs. Unsworth. "Well, I've enjoyed myself today. And I've enjoyed meeting you Thelma. I'm pleased somebody is interested in hearing about

100

our past."

Then she put her hand on Thelma's arm and said, "You're not going to write a book about us, are you love?"

"Well, I might. I've really enjoyed listening to you."

"Thank you very much. If that's the sort of thing you want to know about, you should come to our house and meet my next door neighbour old Tom. He's turned ninety. He used to be a collier. He can tell a few tales about the old days when he worked down the pit. He was buried once at the old Monty. He was lucky to get out alive. Bring Alan with you and I'll show you a few things I've had a long time, some old papers and that. Mrs. Holding will tell you where I live. Just at the top of Frances Street."

And then she proceeded to give everybody a little hug and walked out of the house muttering, "What a lovely spread, what a lovely little spread."

"Well, Thelma, I think they quite enjoyed talking to you," said Granny as they both sat down in the living room a few minutes later. "I've never seen Mrs. Unsworth so lively for a long time. It was a really nice afternoon but I'm tired now. Are you? I don't normally have whisky in tea. It gives me palpitations. I wonder what happened to Mrs. Leatherbarrow?"

"Did she work on the pit brow as well?"

"Oh, no, her mother used to take washing in, and Phyllis, that's her first name, Phyllis used to help her. I don't think you would have learned anything interesting from her. No, it was probably a good thing she didn't come. The others wouldn't have talked so easily. She would have kept changing the subject. She always does."

Half an hour later Grandad came back into the house and when he walked into the living room he found his wife and his lodger sprawled out fast asleep.

17
JOINING THE UNION

It didn't take long before Mr. Williams began to involve himself in the day running of the factory. And just like Cyril, he began to interfere in things he knew little or nothing about. As a result he soon became known as a meddler. But unlike Cyril, who would sulk if he didn't get his own way, Mr. Williams would never take no for an answer. That was why Basil had chosen him and not his brother.

As a young man he had spent time in the States, where he had come under the influence of R. J. Turnbull Junior, author of the thesis "Capitalism, Morals, Individuals and Profits". Combining Weberian sociology with Old Testament Christianty, Turnbull demonstrated, at least to his own satisfaction, that modern man could only be understood as a self-centred individual, not as a social product of his environment. In his view man went to work as much to develop his personal creativity as to receive financial reward. His writings ranted against organisations that attempted to develop what he called a "common-ness among the uncommon". All group associations restricted the freedom of the individual to pursue his own interests, and trade unions in particular were the creation of the Devil. In his last chapter he emphasised how the entire moral basis of the capitalist system was justified in the old Biblical phrase, "the rich man in his castle, the poor man at his gate".

Mr. Williams frequently referred to what he called JT's wordly vision at his Monday briefings when he exhorted the managers to achieve higher levels of output than were physically possible. References from obscure American sociologists were often thrown in, along with the old faithfuls of increasing efficiency, improving time-keeping, removing lines of demarcation and turning off the lights when the sun was shining. Every now and again he would come out with such gems as "All work and no play. That's the way to make them earn their pay." But essentially they served to divert attention from his main aim, which was to reduce the size of the work force and increase output.

Then came his bombshell. Job Evaluation was to be introduced among the staff. Mr Williams knew that the shop floor was well organised into six trade unions. Dark Satanic forces would appear to have a firm grip among the hourly paid, but the staff were a different kettle of fish. That was where he would start to apply what he had learned from his stay in California.

102

As soon as it became known that he wanted to do away with their annual wage increase, there was uproar. Everywhere small groups could be seen discussing the issue. This was Len's big chance. He organised a meeting for the following evening in the Horse and Jockey and spent the day going round finding out who was going to come. Nearly everybody he spoke to said they were, but then with some of them, he would believe it when he saw it. He was to be pleasantly suprised. All the electrical draughtsmen were there except for Stan, over half of the Mechanical section, three work study engineers, two planners and Henry Mather from the Research Laboratory. As soon as they had all settled down he began.

"I've called this meeting to discuss getting the union started. Now that Basil is in charge, the writing is on the wall. You all know what he's like. And with his sidekick coming out with all this bullshit, who knows where it's going to end."

There was a general murmur of approval and nodding of heads. The only noise came from Tommy Litherland and two fitters from the Machine Shop playing dominoes in the tap room.

"Now what has upset most people is his proposal to do away with the annual wage increase and replace it with Job Evaluation. It's hardly suprising that he has started with the staff because he knows he can walk all over us if he wants to."

"The Staff Association won't stand for it," said Dickie.

"You must be joking," shouted out Ken Backhouse.

"I am."

"Exactly. If we leave it to that lot you can kiss goodbye to your increase now. Maurice King has already said he agrees with Job Evaluation and we all know what Norman Kay is like." Nobody made any comment. They all knew how Norman ran the Staff Association as though it was his own personal business.

"Now I know that some of you think it isn't worth us starting a union here because Wilkinson's are not a federated company. Well neither are Mather's and their draughtsmen are in the union. In fact, I heard last week they have just agreed to pay five bob if you've got your ONC and another seven and six for HNC."

"They recognise the shop floor unions here. What's the problem. They'll just have to recognise us," said Yorky.

"Why will they?" asked Colin Dagnall. "They don't have to if they don't want to."

"They will do if we encourage them. You see the situation at the moment is in our favour. Look how busy we are. Half of us are on that Kowloon job. We've got four control panels for Aberthaw to do before the shutdown and another one for Thorpe Marsh. You mechanical lads can speak for yourselves. How long have you been on that blast furnace job? And you've still got the coal handling plant at Bickershaw to finish."

Mick held his hand up to say that he had just heard from John Lynch in the Sales

Office that the firm had just won a repeat order from the Indian State Railways.

"Need I say anymore. You all know how big a job the first order was."

"That's only because you sparkys cocked it up right at the start," said John Meredith. A few laughed but Len said nothing. It was true. He had misunderstood one of the sheet metal drawings and laid out a control panel with its instruments facing the wall. He ignored John's comment and said, "If we play our cards right we could have them by the short and curlies. With all this work in, it's an ideal time to get the union started. Now's the time to strike while the iron's hot."

"I might have known it. We haven't even joined yet and Len is talking about us going out on strike. Well, if that's the case, you can count me out. Strikes never did anybody any good. We'll finish up worse off than we are now."

It was George Pennington, head of the Jig and Tool section. He was the official office moaner. He would regularly moan about the management, the Staff Association, the Government and the local Council. But whenever somebody was prepared to do something positive he would be the first to pour cold water. He had been one of the few people not to sign Alan's petition.

"I was just speaking metaphorically George. I wasn't meaning that we should all go on strike over the Job Evaluation."

"Maybe you aren't Len, but if the full time union man from Liverpool gets involved he'll have us all out - he's a right trouble maker, that Glover."

It was Ernie Broadbent. Everybody knew that as soon as George had spoken, Ernie would follow. He was often called The Pennington Echo.

Len knew it would be a waste of time trying to talk any sense into Ernie so he pitched his reply at some of the older ones who tended to be swayed by George.

"Look Ernie, it'll be up to us what we do. We'll have organised meetings not like the Staff Association. We'll discuss things properly and at the end we'll take a vote and abide by the majority view. Yes, we will ask Ken Glover for his advice, but whether we act upon it will be up to us."

Then, as expected, it was the turn of the third member of the Jig and Tool, Harry Fillingham. "That's all very well, Len, but what happens when the Union has one of its national days of action and we all get called out over some piddling little dispute in Scarborough or Timbuktoo. Will we have to come out even if a majority of us don't want to? And another thing too, I don't agree with supporting that Nelson Mandela. He's just a terrorist. Anyway, what's South Africa got to do with us?"

Then up jumped Dickie. "I don't know why you Jig and Fool men are here. We've all come to discuss joining the union and all you can talk about is not joining it. Well if you're happy with the Staff Association then stay in it. But if you don't want to talk about the union, it's a free country, so piss off."

Then Tony shouted, "Throw them out, they're only trouble makers. The only union they should be in is the Mother's Union." Everybody burst out laughing again as he went on, "If we do let them join, they'll only be the weak link."

Ray Hewitt then indicated he wanted to speak. "When I first worked at Hilton's the wages were right low. We were always complaining, but the firm never did anything. But as soon as we joined the union and brought Ken Glover down it was amazing how soon they started coughing up. He'll soon sort Williams out."

Keith Sanderson said that there were other benefits to being in the union. It had won his brother-in-law one hundred pounds compensation after he had had an accident at Mather's. A few more spoke and John Meredith said that he was still in the AEU. Could he transfer? Then Alan said that he and Tony were still in the Electricians Union, could they do the same?

"We'll leave details like that till later. Look, the time's getting on, I suggest we have a show of hands to see if we've a majority." But before any vote could be taken up jumped George again. "I'll vote to join, but only if it's going to be a union for draffies. I won't join if any Tom, Dick or Harry can be a member."

"You never said that about the Staff Association," shouted Dickie.

"Does that mean you won't let me join?" asked Tony Ellison, one of the planners.

"And what about me, George?" It was Frank Renilson, a Work Study man.

"I didn't mean it literally. I don't object to technical people like you, far from it. After all, your work is closely bound up with the drawing office."

Ernie intervened to try and help his section leader, but he only made matters worse. "What George means is that it should just be a union for draughtsmen, and other technical people: project engineers, research staff, checkers, designers. We don't want it full of old women, do we?"

Len grimaced and said: "I'm sorry but I forgot to mention it. We had two apologies for this meeting. Neil Birchall, one of the installation engineers. He's working at Agecroft. He said that about twenty of the O.C.D are interested in joining. Will they be alright George?" Before he could reply Len went on to say that Joan Watson had gone to the dentists but would call in before the end of the meeting.

"Why is she wanting to join a draughtsman's union? She's not a draughtsman."

"Neither is Tony, or Henry or Neil Birchall. You're not objecting to them being members, are you Ernie?"

"Yes, I know that Len, but she's a woman."

"Your powers of observation have improved considerably," joked Alan.

"What have you got against women anyway?" asked Keith Sanderson. "You're married to one, you've got two daughters and a grand daughter and you probably had a mother once."

"When I was at Hilton's, the women members were our strongest weapon." It was Ray Hewitt again. "Whenever us draughtsmen went on a work to rule, it would be weeks before we made any impact. But as soon as the two girls who ran the print room joined in, there was chaos within a couple of days."

"It was like that in our place," agreed Bill Riley, "when Thelma went off sick. That's why they had to bring Betty in."

The issue of whether women could join the union had obviously upset some of the mechanical draughtsmen who were now having their own meeting. Charlie stood up and said: "Can I just ask through you Mr. Chairman if George or Ernie will be prepared to tell Joan when she arrives that she can't come in."

They all burst out laughing again. Ernie was a little weasel of a man and George wasn't much bigger. If she wanted to, Big Joan could have lifted the pair of them up off the floor. Charlie's comment quickly took the wind out of their sales and the discussion moved on to the issue of wages.

"I suggest that we tell them we are refusing to take part in any Job Evaluation," suggested John Fox. "And I think we should bang in a wage claim at the same time."

"I'm not sure about that," countered Tony Ellison. "It might be an idea to go along with it for a bit. Let's see what it's like, but I agree we should put a wage claim in."

"Will it be a flat rate increase or a percentage increase" asked Jack Large.

"We'll decide that later," said Len. "First things first. Let's see if we've got a majority. Will you and Charlie count the votes, Alan? So, based on everything that's been said, how many are favour of joining the union?"

Ernie and George abstained, otherwise it was unanimous. Ray Hewitt suggested there should be another meeting to which Ken Glover should be invited.

"How about next Monday, same time same place," suggested Len.

"Hadn't you better check with Glover first," asked George. "These union officials are a law unto themselves. They just won't come running down here for you at such short notice."

"I already have done. Ken's free and so is this room until half past seven. I've also made sure there are no football matches or any mucky films on the box."

The meeting was starting to break up when Jim Fenton said: "I would like to move a vote of thanks to Len for doing such a good job tonight. I must admit I was dubious about joining a union, and particularly this one after all I've heard about it. But from what I've heard so far I'm quite satisfied."

After the meeting had finished, Yorky said to Len: "Put that in the minutes what Jim said, just in case he forgets when he's back in work tomorrow."

"Aye, and put that bit in when Dickie told Ernie to piss off," said Alan. "We'll have to have a new award for quote of the year."

106

"I like the way Tony and Frank stood up when George said it should only be a union for draughtsmen. You couldn't have done better if you'd planned it."

"Well actually, Keith, I did plan it. I knew he would say something like that so I warned Tony and Frank this morning."

As they were chatting, Tommy Litherland came over. "Hi boss, what are you lot up to, plotting the revolution?"

As soon as Len told him, Tommy suprised them by asking if he could join. "Give us some leaflets and I'll pass them round. There's a lot of supervisors who might be interested as well. We're all getting pissed off with Williams."

Alan and Charlie started to count numbers. Anything up to thirty draughtsmen, six Work Study men, four planners, maybe a dozen from the Lab, twenty from O.C.D. and the supervisors. Then there were the estimators in the main Office, the Technical Publicity people and those in the Measurements Laboratory. Until recently the union had been known as the Association of Engineering and Ship-building Draughtsmen. Now that it was called the Draughtsmen's and Allied Technicians Association, a much wider range of technical staff could join it. Things looked promising. They estimated they could soon have over a hundred members.

"Will Thelma want to join, Alan?" asked Tony Ellison.

"I'm sure she will. I've got an application form for her. I'll give it to her tomorrow night."

"When's she coming back?"

"Pretty soon. You'll hardly recognise her. She must have put on nearly half a stone."

"Oh, aye. I wonder why," and all the others laughed as Yorky started humming the Wedding March.

"No, its not that, it's my Granny's cooking that's done it."

"That's a new explanation for it," laughed Tommy.

"So, is she all right now? She must have been pretty ill?"

"She was. They almost took her to hospital. But she wouldn't have got any better treatment there than she got from my Granny."

"Is she going to carry on living there?"

"Yes."

"I'm not being funny Alan, but is she still wearing them same clothes?"

"Listen Tony, when I went down to where she lived before to get her things, I was amazed just how little she had."

"Has she still got that thin green coat? However she kept warm in that I'll never know."

Then Brian Watt chipped in. "You know I feel really bad about her. It was me that nicknamed her the little Welsh dresser. If I'd known about her situation, she could have had some of our Janet's stuff."

"I remember when she started in our office," said Bill Riley. "She looked thrown together, but she was a good worker, I'll say that for her."

"She worked for me after that," said Tony. "She was alright at first but after a month I kept finding her in the Print Room. I'm afraid I had to tell her off a few times. I feel pretty bad about how I treated her now. You can tell her she can go and see Joan as much as she wants when she comes back."

"It wasn't Joan she was going to see, Tony. She was trying to bump into yon man," explained Charlie, nodding towards Alan.

"The thing that amazes me about it all, how was it that none of us knew a blind bit about her before she fell ill? How long had she been here, it must have been the best part of six months. Even Joan couldn't get much out of her, and she knows something about everybody else in this place."

"I don't think she wanted anybody to know, Len," said Bill. "You could hardly get a word out of her sometimes. Maybe we know why now."

"Did you not know anything about her then, Alan? You used to talk to her enough."

"Not really. She'd talk about everything but herself."

"Well, I'll be glad when she does come back," said Bill. "She's the best girl we've had and there's been a few over the years."

"Eh, guess who I saw in Earlestown last Saturday pushing a pram" said Tony. "That gormless one from Hemsley, the one that looked like Helen Shapiro."

"Aye, and she sounded like Billy Eckstein when she opened her mouth. Don't remind me of her. The day she started was the day my hair started falling out. She was a walking disaster, that one."

One by one they began to leave. By the time Alan caught his bus it was turned half past ten. As he walked down Parry Lane he was glad to see that Edith's chip shop was still open. Within minutes he was sat in the living room devouring a large fish, double chips and mushy peas. Eight hours later his mum came downstairs to find the light still on and her youngest son fast asleep on the settee, still wearing his donkey jacket and scarf and the scattered remains of his supper strewn all over the carpet.

18

THE WALL GOES UP: THE WALL COMES DOWN

Alan expected to find them all discussing the previous night's meeting when he walked in. But the place was unusually quiet. They all had their heads down and he could immediately see why. Mr. Williams was in John Battesby's office with Mick in heated discussion.

"What's up Charlie? What's he doing here?"

"It's something to do with that job in the foundry. There's been some almighty cock-up by the sound of it. I can't work out who's to blame, but I think Lurch is involved in it."

For years the Foundry basement had served as a home for unwanted castings. But now it had been decided to divide it into two, turn the top half into a high voltage test laboratory and put the electrical switchgear in the bottom half. Mick had been given the drawing work to do, not an easy task since he had to deal with the Foundry Manager Frank Day, a man well known for changing his mind. As a result despite, and Mick's efforts, the job soon began to drag.

Unknown to either Frank or Mick, Arthur Wood had begun to stick his nose in. He kept telling Mr. Williams that unless the new laboratory was operating by the time of the Works Shutdown, they would be unable to handle the increased workload that was expected in September. And in his view, the reason for the delay lay with the drawing office.

Finally Mr.Williams decided he had heard enough of it. Guided by what he had read in 'Capitalism, Morals, Individuals and Profits' he acted. His mentor, R.J.Turnbull Junior, had written that top level decisions had to be made in an environment that was uncluttered by the minutiae of oppressive detail and unaffected by the subjectivism of those directly involved.

On Friday afternoon he issued instructions for a dividing wall between the two halves of the basement to be built over the weekend. This would force the pace and if Mick Henderson was not up to it, then the job would have to be given to someone else.

As he ate his breakfast that morning, Mick thought about the day ahead, which would be spent supervising the installation of two large motors that were being delivered from Trafford Park. As soon as he arrived in work, he would have to go to the foundry, which would be a pity since he would miss all the chat about what had happened at the meeting.

When the first lorry arrived, the gateman, Vince, stepped into the cab and directed the driver to the foundry and through the double doors into the basement. As they drove in, Vince, who had been off a few days, saw the wall for the first time.

"What the hell is that?"

"It's a wall, my friend. A new one by the look of it. We've got them all over Salford."

"Do you know where this load is supposed to go?"

"No, but I feel sure you're going to tell me."

"On the other side of that wall."

"You mean I've got to back out of here?"

"No. This is the only way into the place. Wait here. I'll have to tell the Foundry Manager. He can sort this out. He gets paid enough."

As soon as Frank Day heard the news he rang Mr.Williams. It was also the first that Frank had heard about the wall, having been on holiday on Friday. Within ten minutes Mr.Williams was storming down to the drawing office. Aware of how he operated and of the way Frank would sometimes deny having changed his mind, Mick had kept a careful record of every thing that had been agreed between them. As soon as Mr.Williams began to imply that it was Mick's fault, Mick was able to show him that it wasn't.

Mr.Williams did not stay long. He made one phone call and then disappeared. The next sighting of him was in the basement ten minutes later with the building fore-man George Shuttleworth, and where he was heard to say:

"I know the wall hasn't been up a day. I don't care. Just do what I tell you. Knock the effing thing down."

As soon as he had left, Yorky said:

"Our's is not to reason why. It's up to us to draw and then modify."

Len smiled and replied:

"I don't think that would've been a good time to ask him for a meeting to discuss our wage claim."

Everybody gathered round Mick as he came out of John Battesby's office, saying to no one in particular and everybody in general, "Manager. He couldn't manage a hot dinner." They all waited while he went back to his board, sat on his stool and explained what had happened.

"You know the only one way to get anything big into the basement is through the double doors at the top. Well, thanks to Lurch and his interfering, Williams told George Shuttleworth to build a dividing wall over the weekend, so now the only way into the bottom half is through the door in the pattern stores."

"You haven't designed a switchroom with no access, have you Mick?"

"Give me some credit, Greeno. When I'd got everything in place I was going to tell George to build that wall and at the same time put double doors in the north wall at the far end. But he couldn't do that before I get that old A.E.I. panel moved. And I can't do that until we've installed the new panel up near where Elmo the Mighty used to have his cutting machine. As far as I was concerned it was all organised. It would have been alright if Lurch hadn't interfered. He's always been the same, wanting everything done yesterday."

"I thought he'd got you in there because he thought you were the new union man," laughed Alan.

At this, Stan pipped up: "What happened last night at the meeting? I'm sorry I couldn't make it. The wife was ill."

"So are we," said Tony. "You let us down. We lost. They voted to stay in the Staff Association."

"You must be joking!"

"It's alright Stan, he's only winding you up. They all voted to join except for Ernie and George. We're having another meeting next Monday," and then began a discussion about what they thought should be done next.

It carried on until they were joined by Tommy Wiseman and Billy Watson from the Electrical Wiring shop. News about the meeting had already circulated around the supervisors and both indicated they were interested. As they were talking Big Joan walked into the office and when he saw her, Billy said loudly:

"I'll agree to join as long as it's not full of old women."

"Don't say we're going to have that one all over again?"

"Don't get upset Len. I'll join it if it's full of young ones."

Then, turning to Joan he said: "Have I got to call you Sister Watson now?"

She laughed at him as she hit him on the shoulder. She was married to his younger brother, in other words his sister-in-law at home and now one of the sisters at work. As he put his arm round her and started telling them how lucky their Jim was, the phone rang. It was George Shuttleworth warning them that Williams was on his way back to the Drawing Office. Tommy and Billy decided to leave straightaway, soon to be followed by Mick. Unfortunately he couldn't get out quick enough and they came back together. They discussed the job again and Mick agreed that as soon as he had all the details he could finish the work off within a couple of days.

"Eh, it's tough at the top," said Dickie as soon as Williams was out of sight.

"I know, but it's a damn sight tougher at the bottom," remarked Mick, "but I know where I would rather be."

"Isn't Lurch a complete pillock?"

"I'll tell you what Sam, I think that Mick's odds on favourite for the Holder of the Golden Pencil," said Charlie

"How can we have it if Lurch doesn't work here any more."

"It doesn't matter, Greeno. As long as he's working at Wilkinson's, we'll have it."

"I think Malcom Heaton is in with a chance," said Len. "Did you hear what happened on Saturday night?"

"No."

"Lurch went out with the Railway gang to check up on the lads who test those new PTFE insulators every month. He thinks there's only enough work for one of them. Do you know what I'm on about?"

"No. I always thought the Railway gang were a bunch of cowboys who robbed trains in the Wild West."

"Very funny, Greeno. It's Stan Pilkington's lot. They travel at night in those special railway wagons. You must have seen them. You can stand on the roof and inspect the overhead wires as the train is going along. I thought you'd be on it.

"Anyway, it was about half five and they had nearly finished when Mal sees Lurch walk over to some bushes and start having a pee. They've got this bell system in each carriage, press once to tell the driver at the front to start and two to stop. So Mal presses the bell and off the train goes. Lurch had to leg it back to the depot at Stockport in the rain. When he got back, he had a right go at Malcom until Stan told him it was his own fault. If he wanted to go to the toilet, he had to ask permission. I don't think he'll be going out with them again."

"Why didn't one of the lads in the first carriage press the stop button?"

"Would you have done?"

"No."

"Well, there's your answer."

They summoned up enough enthusiasm to start work, but it wasn't long before they were stopped by the arrival of the tea trolley.

As soon as they had bought their teas, Dickie said, "So, what's the next move, Len? What does our great leader suggest?"

"The first thing we've to do is elect an office committee and a C.M."

"What's that?"

"C.M. It stands for Corresponding Member. It's his job to collect the subs each week and distribute the Union Vacancy List and the DATA Journal."

"Yes, but what are we going to do about the Job Evaluation, and are we going to

112

put in for a wage claim?"

"The first thing is, we'll have to get them to agree to negotiate with us. They won't like it, but they don't have a lot of choice. They already recognise the shop floor unions."

"But what if they don't? They wouldn't recognise DATA at that firm in Scarborough, would they? They were out on strike for months over it."

"It won't come to that here, Stan. They've far too much to lose with all these orders that are coming in. I think if Williams is clever he will probably say that we can only represent draughtsmen."

"Is that what R.J.Turnbull Junior would say?"

"I don't know. They don't have his books in our library, Mick."

"So what do we do if he does say that we can only represent draughtsmen."

"We'll just have to put a bit of pressure on him. But the main thing is we'll all have to stick together. We don't want George or Ernie dividing us up before we've even started."

"Solidarity brothers!" shouted out Tony raising his clenched fist high in the air.

"And what about the sisters?" asked Rita, who had just walked in.

"It's all for one and one for all. That's right isn't it Brother Len?"

"That's right, Rita. It's a very simple lesson, but it's suprising how many have never learned it. If we all stick together, the sky's the limit."

"Well, we'll see," said Stan. "I can remember 1926."

"That's because they didn't stick together," remarked Len. But before they could continue, in walked Frank Day. An hour later, and within hearing range of seven other witnesses, he agreed that the very first layout that Mick had drawn was the one he wanted.

19
THE MYSTERY VOICE

By lunch time the following day they had organised the Office Committee, made up of Ray Hewitt, Henry Mather, Ken Stott, an estimator, Bill Finney from O.C.D., with Len as C.M. Their first task was to see John Walker, the Personnel Manager, about formal recognition of the union.

"No use talking to me about things like that Len," were John's first comments. "I'll go and have a word with Williams. He's running the whole show now. I sometimes wonder why I bother to come in these days."

Ten minutes later he was back. "I've talked to the Great White Chief, Len. His exact words to me were, 'If they want to be in a union, they can all go home now!' You can take that which ever way you want to. But remember this, he likes to have his instructions carried out to the letter."

"It looks as though we're going to have a battle on our hands straight away," said Len as they walked away.

"Far from it. I think he's just scored an own goal."

"How do you work that one out, Ray?"

"He said if we want to be in a union, which we do, then we've got to show him. And the way he wants us to show him is by going home now."

"That's a convoluted way of looking at it."

"Look, Len, like John Walker said, you've got to carry out his instructions to the letter."

"Yes, I know that but ....".

"There's no but about it. He's given us an ideal opportunity to flex our muscles. It's turned three now we've got to act fast. Let's have a committee meeting."

Len was not too sure if this was the right course of action, but the rest of the committee agreed with Ray.

"Will there be any problems with your lads, Henry?"

"Not at all. Lurch is making our life a misery. This'll be one way of showing him we're all fed up."

"What about O.C.D. Bill?"

"We'll have to forget the lads who are working out. But the rest will be out like a shot. They're all up in arms about his plan to reduce our out of town allowance."

"We might have a bit of a problem with our lot," said Ken. "I was suprised when some of them joined in the first place".

"I know what to do. Henry, get all your members to come out the back way and walk down past Jack Cunliffe's place. Tell them to make plenty of noise when they go past the offices. That should help them make up their minds."

"And I know what we'll do," said Len. "We'll start at our end and walk past all those weak-kneed, yellow-bellied mechanical lot and then we'll go through the Work Study."

"You're learning fast," laughed Ray.

"You're a bit of a dark horse, aren't you? I only brought you in to make up the numbers."

"Don't worry Len. I won't tell anybody you were going to cave in right from the word go."

"As they walked into the office Len shouted out: "It gives me very great pleasure to say this. Everybody out!""

"What's up? Are we not having a meeting first?"

"No, there's no time Mick. Williams has told us if we want to be in a union, then we've got to show him by going home. If we don't get a move on we'll be doing it in our own time."

Suprisingly there was no opposition and the office emptied as quickly as though it was going home time. Fortunately, two of the Jig and Tool section were on holiday, one had gone to the dentists and Ernie was in the toilets at the time. He must have had quite a shock when he came back to a deserted office.

Everybody was in early the following morning, even Alan. Soon Len got the expected phone call from Miss Place summoning him to see the boss. He and Ray returned twenty minutes later, just as Joan was pouring the teas out.

"So, was he pleased to see we'd come back?"

"To put it mildly Charlie, no. If it was up to him, we would now be on our way to Australia. He just went on and on. According to him we were outside the law; we weren't a recognised body; we hadn't given seven days notice; we hadn't had a vote and, best of all, we might be held responsible if any penalty clauses are invoked because we weren't working normally."

"What, for a whole half hour?"

"So what's the outcome then. Where do we go from here?"

"As far as he's concerned, Job Evaluation is still on whether we like it or not. And his other instructions to us lot was to stop thinking we were God's gift to Wilkinson's."

"What do you mean?"

"Draughtsmen are employed to draw. That's all we should do. He's sick and tired of us trying to run the place."

"What's he on about?"

"What he doesn't really understand is how we work. He really thinks all draughtsmen should do is draw," said Ray.

"Well what else are we paid to do?"

"Eh, hang on a minute Mick, how much time do you spend in the foundry?"

"It's only to get information I need to make sure what I draw is right."

"Exactly, but he thinks you don't need to do that."

"Well, he's a fool."

"Do you know what he said? Every time he goes in the factory he sees a draughtsman trying to get out of drawing," Ray laughed and went on, imitating Williams's accent as he did so.

"Yesterday I walked past the Wiring shop and I saw Holroyd wiring a contactor. I went through the machine shop and I saw Meredith instructing a lathe operator how to use his machine, and to cap it all I saw Henderson in the foundry driving the crane."

It was true. Mick was still laying out all the equipment for the modernisation of the iron foundry. Part of his task was to run a cable up to a junction box in the roof. The best vantage point to see where to do this was from the crane driver's cabin. While he was up there, Harry, the new driver, asked him if he fancied driving the thing. Of course Mick said yes. It was only for a minute up and down the shop. It was just unfortunate that Mr. Williams was walking through the foundry at the time.

"So, Clever Dick thinks we should spend all day drawing and never going into the factory," said Stan. "The man is a pillock."

"Exactly," said Ray, "he's just scored another own goal."

"How do you mean?"

"Call an office committee Len, and I'll tell you."

At their lunch time meeting, they listened as Len reported back and then Ray came up with his suggestion:

"Play him at his own game. That's the way to deal with him. Just do what he's told us to do, but do it literally. That's what we did last night, and it worked. The thing is he told us that the draughtsman's job is to draw. Nothing more, nothing less. No going down on the shop floor to sort things out. Just working to instructions provided. So that's what we'll do."

"What good will that do?"

"It'll be a work to rule, his rules. We'll cripple them within a week. I guarantee it."

"How can you be sure?"

"I can't, but it always worked when we were at Mathers."

But it didn't quite work to their advantage at Wilkinson's, well not at first. The

116

draughtsmen spent all day in front of their drawing boards and wasted little time swanning around the factory. Their output actually went up and they were not too happy when they heard what Williams thought about it.

It was Joan, the source of all information, who told them on Friday morning as she poured out the teas. "Mr. Williams seems to be very pleased with the new arrangement, you lot drawing all day. He hopes you'll have found some more rules to obey by the time he gets back."

"How do you always know what's going on here?"

"It's suprising what you hear on this job, Mick."

"I reckon it must be something you put in the tea."

"I know one thing," said Yorky. "I'm getting right brassed off having to spend all day here with you lot."

"He hasn't seen Big Bertha all week, that's what's annoying him," laughed Dickie.

"Well, she is a sight for sore eyes, and she's got a soft spot for me."

"If she fancies you, it must be her that's got the sore eyes."

"If she fancies Yorky we'd better start calling her Blind Bertha."

After Joan had gone, Dickie said: "I think it might be a good idea if we do what Williams wants and find another rule to obey."

"Like what?"

"If you look in the old Drawing Office handbook, you know, what we used to call Fraser's Bible, it says that at the end of each working day all drawings should be returned to the Print Room."

"That'll waste at least three minutes."

"Yes, and what about in the morning, Mick. If you go by the book it says that draughtsmen aren't permitted to go looking for drawings. You're supposed to fill out a form and wait while one of the girls gets your drawing out for you. And then you're supposed to enter the details in the Drawings Out Register."

"Another five minutes wasted, that should really bring the place grinding to a halt."

"Yes, but if you multiply five minutes by thirty, that means the last draughtsman won't get hold of his drawings for at least an hour and a half. And if Rita has been on the razzle the night before, she'll hardly be wanting to work flat out for that length of time, will she?"

And so, just before finishing time, over a hundred drawings, some of which had been 'missing' for weeks, were put down on the Print Room counter. And the following Monday morning, they all queued up as Joan and Rita slowly worked their way through an enormous pile of drawings.

By the end of the week the output from the drawing office was well down. But what Mr. Williams thought about it was unknown since no one had seen him for days. And it was also around this time that the Mystery Voice appeared on the scene.

By now Mr Williams was well known for the way he sent his instructions out over the phone. He would just say something like, "Williams here, I want you to do this, that and the other. Any problems," and before there was time for his foreman or whoever to question him, he would slam the phone down. There was no discussion, it was nothing less than a command from on high.

As a result, during the course of the week, instructions were relayed to many of the foremen. Most seemed a little strange, even bizarre, but the general consensus of opinion was that an important visitor was due to make an appearance.

They finally discovered where Williams was when Joan told them that he was in India and in her words had just won an order for some "railway electrocution equipment".

As they were walking up to the canteen, Yorky asked Alan: "If you were a Managing Director and were on the other side of the world, would you ring your foremen up in the middle of the night just to tell them to tidy up the place?"

"I don't suppose I would."

"I was talking to Billy Tunstall in the car park last night. He doesn't think it's Williams. He reckons somebody is impersonating him."

"Who?"

"He thinks it might be Charlie, but I don't know why he would want to do that."

"No, it can't be Charlie. I know he can take Williams off to a tee, but he's never out of the office. We'd know if it was him, where could he phone from?"

"Exactly. Don't say anything to anybody, but keep your eyes open."

The following Monday, Williams reappeared. By this time a large amount of warehouse stock, redundant machinery and scrap metal had been moved around the factory from one resting place to another. In addition, the old apprentice shop which was due for knocking down in the summer if it had not fallen down by then had been re-painted.

But when Williams did reappear he had far more important things on his plate. One of his first actions was to call all the senior foremen to his office.

"I'm pleased to tell you we've won a large order from the Far East. It looks as though we'll have to start a night shift in the brass foundry. We'll have to put back that proposed shut down on number three kiln and we'll have to get the old rolling mill running again for the T4 ingots. The reason I've brought you here is to find out if you can see any problems on the shop floor. We can't afford any bottlenecks or holds ups. Not on this job. There is a lot of money involved."

They discussed the general situation and after a while Ronnie Garner asked if there

118

would be any design changes.

"Yes, I was going to ask John Battesby to join us. There'll be quite a bit to re-design for the speed control units, but I believe he's gone to Sutton Manor this morning."

"Well, there is one problem you'll have to deal with. There's hardly a drawing coming out of the D.O. at the moment."

"Don't tell me those silly buggers are still behaving like school kids. I'd sack them all if I could."

"I think it might be more constructive to sit round the table and discuss their grievances. From what I hear, all they want is to have their union treated like any other union here."

"You're not one of their members are you?" But before Ronnie could find a suitable answer, Williams went on: "Yes, I'll have to get it sorted out when I get back on Friday. I've got to meet Basil in London tomorrow."

At lunchtime Billy made a point of seeing Yorky again.

"I was right. It wasn't Williams who kept ringing up last week."

"How do you know?"

"Well, after we'd finished our meeting I asked him what India was like. It turned out where they were staying they had some bad floods. He said there was no power on for two days and all the telephone lines were down.

So then I said, tongue in cheek, "So you didn't have chance to ring here and check what we were all doing in your absence?" Do you know what his reply was?

"I never used a telephone all the time I was there."

"So you were right. Somebody was impersonating him while he was away. Who could it have been and why?"

But it was going to be a long time before anybody found out.

20

THE WORKS DANCE

There were eight of them sat in the Masons Arms in Southport. They were there for Wilkinson's Staff Association Spring Dance. With Alan and Thelma were Ken and Jenny, Ronnie and Dorothy and Geoff and Sally.

Ken had first met Jenny on Christmas Eve in the Co-op Hall. She worked at Hilton's on the assembly line and had a reputation for being fast. In fact, she was so fast she had once represented Lancashire schools in the hundred yards when she was sixteen.

Geoff had been going out with Sally for about three months. She wasn't interested in athletics. If she had been, the shot putt or the discuss would probably have been her event. She was a real laugh. Her family had moved down from Silloth when she was thirteen and her accent showed it, a combination of West Cumbria and South Lancashire.

Dorothy and Ronnie had been in Alan's class at Lane Head school. He remembered her vividly from those days. She was really awful then. No one wanted to sit near her because of the smell. Her clothes were always too small, her teeth were stained and they all said she had nits. Whenever anybody upset her she would kick out at them with her clogs. Alan remembered one afternoon having her as his partner in country dancing and he had to hold her hand. All the boys had laughed at him afterwards and he had gone straight home and had a bath, even though it was only Thursday. She was so different now. Everybody wanted to hold her hand and stand close to her. It was funny her being with Ronnie though. He had been one of her worst tormentors.

It was the first time they had been out as a group. As soon as they had sat down and organised the kitty, Sally asked Thelma, who was sat next to her, if she had been to the Floral Gardens before. On hearing her Welsh accent she said loudly:

"Don't you think they talk funny round here?" At this Ronnie and Geoff began to mimic her Cumberland twang. To anyone sat nearby it probably sounded like the Goon Show.

The first drinks soon went down and, as Ronnie and Alan were at the bar, Geoff asked who was going to Widnes the following day. The conversation moved on to some recent games they had seen, the Good Friday defeat of Wigan, the two matches against Swinton over Easter and last Saturday's win over Featherstone Rovers.

As they were talking, Dorothy said to Thelma, who had hardly said a thing, "Have you not been to watch the Saints yet?" Before she could reply Dorothy went on: "Why don't you come with us next Monday. They're playing Oldham. You'll enjoy it. There'll be a big crowd."

As she spoke, Thelma saw Alan coming back from the bar with a tray of drinks. To show them all she was beginning to pick up their sense of humour, she said:

"Alan, are you going trainspotting on Monday or do you fancy going to the match?"

At this all the others fell about laughing until Ronnie shouted out:

"No, you're wrong Thelma, Monday night is when he does his stamp collecting."

"I'll always remember my first game," reminisced Geoff.

"Who was that against, Broughton Rangers?" inquired Ronnie.

"No. It was against Rochdale, our Chris was playing."

"I didn't know he ever played for the Saints?"

"He didn't. He played for Rochdale."

"Do you remember our first match, Alan?" asked Ken. "Saints won seventy six thirty eight."

"Who were they playing?" asked Jenny "The blind school!".

"No. It was Italy. I've still got the programme at home."

Then it was Ronnie's turn.

"I started watching the Saints when I was seven."

"Seven, you wouldn't be strong enough to push the turnstile round," laughed Sally.

"We didn't pay. We waited until half time when they opened the gates and we went in for nix. We used to go every week, but there was one thing I could never understand. One week there would be thousands of people there. The next week there would only be about a hundred."

"You daft bugger, that was the A team," said Geoff.

"Yes, I know that now. I always liked those games. It was always dead easy to get their autographs."

The conversation moved on to the various grounds they had been to and who had been to the most. Then Thelma asked if anyone had been to any grounds in Wales. They all started to laugh.

"What's up. Have I said something funny. They do play rugby in Wales don't they? I thought they had a good team."

Ronnie tried to put her straight.

"There are two types of rugby, Thelma. Up here, we play Rugby League. In Wales and everywhere else they play Rugby Union."

"What's the difference?" she asked in all innocence. At that point they all began to explain it to her, but this simply made matters worse. And she couldn't make head nor tail of it when Geoff started telling her about the demand for broken time payment in 1895.

"Make a less noise, you lot," said Dorothy. "You just come with us on Monday, Thelma. We'll tell you what's happening on the field and later on we can tell you what the difference is between the two."

"Don't worry if you don't follow it all at first," said Sally. "I went for weeks before I could understand it, but you'll love the atmosphere and all the shouting and the humour."

The conversation carried on in this vein. Thelma didn't follow all of it, but she just loved being part of such a big group of people. She had now come to understand their Lancashire sense of humour and why when they had first met at work, Alan had kept calling her Blodwynn and asking her if she could play the harp. Sometimes it seemed almost childish. Often they would pick up on some feature or physical appearance of one of the others and blow it up out of all proportion.

Dorothy has just started wearing spectacles. Geoff turned to her and said: "I like your new glasses, Dorothy. Do you think you could see your way to lending me a pound?"

Ronnie was sat right in the corner. If he wanted to get out, at least four of them would have to stand up, so he said to Jenny: "Are you still running with Sutton Harriers?" and before she could reply, he went on, "Well could you run to the bar and get me some cigarettes."

The influence of such Lancashire comedians as Ken Platt with his, "I won't take my coat off, I'm not stopping", and Al Read and his, "You're not waiting for a bus there are you love. I wouldn't bother, they don't run down here any more", were obvious. Also, there were the meaningless one liners like the long drawn out use of the name Jennifer, or the number ninety two, taken from the Jimmy Jewel and Ben Warris comedy programme 'Up The Pole'.

They had two more rounds and then it was time to go to the Floral Hall. It was the first dance Thelma had ever been to. As they emerged from the cloakroom who should she see but her boss Brian Butterworth. She hardly recognised him. Gone was that awful suit he always wore, the RAF tie and those brightly polished brown shoes. In their place he was wearing a teddy boy suit, a bootlace tie and a pair of brothel creepers. He introduced Thelma to his wife and then asked her to dance. Before she knew it, they were on the floor and he was going through his rock and roll routine. Many familiar faces passed by. They smiled at her and laughed at him. He always made a fool of himself at the works dance.

As she was making her way off the floor she saw Alan in deep conversation with a young man she didn't know. As soon as Alan saw her he waved her over and said;

"My good lady, I want to introduce you to Lancashire's Marco Polo, international traveller, wit, raconteur, 1948 world marbles champion, our very own Lord Yates of Hemsley."

The two lads were drunk and their speech showed it. Eric began by apologising about Christmas Eve, but Alan soon butted in:

"You don't need to apologise. She's glad you got in instead of me. She thinks you're wonderful, and so do I."

"Well, let me have a dance with you then."

He tried to speak coherently as they shuffled around but it wasn't easy. He was too drunk, but his feelings about Alan were clear. "He's a great lad, Greeno. We've always been mates. He'll not let you down. He's one of the best." When Thelma could finally get a word in she asked him how long he had known Alan.

"Years, ever since we used to go to the baths on a Saturday and we'd leave our bikes in his Granny's yard." He then went back to praising Alan, repeating himself two or three times. Suddenly the music stopped. There was a roll on the drums. It was time for the raffle. They walked back to where Alan was stood. Eric shook his hand, told her again that Alan was one of the best, kissed her and walked away, saying, "Take her to your Granny's sometime Greeno, and tell her I sent you."

As always the draw was made by Norman Kay, the secretary of the Staff Association. It was his annual moment of glory. Despite all that had happened over the Job Evaluation fiasco, Norman still intended giving his usual long boring speech. Just as he was starting his "one, two, three, can you hear me, mother" routine, Big Joan plumped herself down next to Thelma, slapped her on the back and said:

"Hi, pardner. I've just heard you're going to start watching the Saints."

"News travels fast around here. I am, but you'll have to explain some of the rules to me. I don't even know the difference between Rugby League and Rugby Union."

"You don't know the meaning of the word fast until you've seen Tom Van Vollenhoven, our flying winger, but don't worry. Come into the Print Room on Monday and I'll explain the main points. We'll invite Mick as well, with him being a Wiganer, he won't know much about them either."

By now Norman was announcing the winners of the raffle. The third prize was won by Helen Briggs from the Wages Department, and the second prize by Bill Travis, Jack Critchley's new assistant in the Apprentice school. But it was the main winner who provided the biggest laugh of the evening. The number was announced and up to the platform strode Steve Worsley, a foremen in the Assembly Shop, to hear Norman read out that his prize was:

"A trip up the Mersey on the Royal Iris and a fabulous meal for you and the lady of your choice."

Steve's partner might well be his wife with whom he had spent the evening, but it equally could have been Janet who worked in the Senior Staff canteen and with whom Steve had been carrying on with for years, known by just about everybody in Ashurst, other than his wife and her husband.

As the dancing re-started, Joan grabbed hold of Alan and propelled him onto the dance floor. Geoff took Thelma's arm and they followed. As they waltzed round they noticed a very smart woman with long blonde hair glide past. Then, as they were walking off the floor, they were confronted by this Diana Dors lookalike. She stood in front of them and said: "Thelma, Thelma Johnson. My God whatever are you doing here? I can't believe it!"

Neither could Thelma. She hadn't the faintest clue who the woman was.

"Thelma. Don't you know me? I'm Gwen from the home. Don't you remember? Me, you, Sandra and Beth. I'm Gwen Walker."

Quickly Thelma's thoughts went back to that unhappy time in her life. She remembered Sandra. She was her best friend, her only real friend. Yes there was a girl called Beth, tall and thin with a persistent rasping cough and the other girl. No, it couldn't be, she was a plump dumpling of a girl with glasses held together with sticking plaster and dark hair.

But it was. Once the shock was over they began talking thirteen to the dozen. After a few minutes Gwen pointed to Geoff and asked, "Is this your man?"

"No, he's over by the bandstand. This is one of his friends."

"Come on. Take me over to meet him. My God, after all this time and haven't you changed. I only just recognised you. Aren't you looking well?"

Gwen was nearly fourteen when she had been put in the home. When she left two years later she looked nineteen. By the time she was nineteen she was married to a young miner. Six months later he was killed in a roof fall. Shortly afterwards she left the area and before the year was out had married again into a farming family in North Wales.

"What are you doing here?"

"It's through Paul. He's a sales engineer for Wilkinson's. He always gets invited to these dances." Then Gwen took Alan's hand and said, "Let me dance with your man. He looks nice."

As soon as they stepped onto the dance floor Gwen said: "Thelma looks a lot happier than when I last saw her. Somebody must be looking after her."

"She's been living with my Granny and Grandad since Christmas. It must be the best place she's ever lived. She loves living there. They treat her like royalty."

"I can tell that. You know she had a tough time in that home. She was so small then. She always got pushed around by some of the bigger ones and she never seemed to get enough to eat, poor kid."

"She's eating like a horse now. She must have put on a stone since she's been there."

"Has she got many friends? That's what she always wanted to have, lots of friends. She didn't have many down there. I always felt so sorry for her."

"She does now. They all like her at work."

"I often wondered what would happen to her. I'm glad she's got somewhere nice to live. She deserves it."

As the dance finished, her husband Paul joined them and said: "We'll have to get back to our table Gwen. I want you to meet my new boss."

"It's been great to see you Thelma. Please keep in touch." Then Gwen wrote her address on a scrap of paper and as she walked away she commented: "I like your man, he's nice." With that, as suddenly as Gwen had burst back into Thelma's life, she departed.

Thelma was now exhausted by it all. She took Alan's hand and they sat down. He put his arm around her and she snuggled up beside him. What an action packed evening it had been: the journey on the coach, all the laughing and joking in the pub, the drinks she had had, dancing with Brian Butterworth, meeting Eric Yates and then Gwen. A few sad memories passed through her head. She thought about Sandra. She had been her best friend, really her only friend, and then one afternoon when she had come home from school, Sandra had gone. She hadn't even said goodbye. Why, and where was she now?

She sat there watching the world go by. She really had enjoyed herself even though she hadn't a clue about how to do the steps. She looked at Alan and smiled. He was asleep. She looked across to the dance floor and saw Ken and Jenny glide by. She decided to close her eyes for a minute. Then she'd wake him up and they would have their first dance together.

Suddenly there was a flash and a lot of noise. They both woke with a start. The lights were on, the band had finished and everybody was stood there wearing their coats.

"What a pair," Ken said, "What a pair of dreamers. It's all over. Time to go." And as she struggled to get up, Thelma saw Ronnie giving a ten shilling note to a man with a large camera.

She remembered getting on the coach in Southport but little about the journey back to Ashurst. She vaguely remembered getting off outside the Town Hall and walking past the Baths. The next thing she saw was the sun streaming through her bedroom window. She was lying on her bed still wearing her coat and one shoe. She struggled downstairs and saw Alan sat in the kitchen gingerly drinking black coffee and nibbling at a piece of toast.

"Good morning, madam," Granny said. "How are you? You look terrible."

"Fine," she croaked.

Granny laughed: "You know where the aspirins are. Have a couple and I'll make you some breakfast."

Shortly after Alan left.

"I'll come round after tea Thelma. I'm off to the match this afternoon."

"Well, you'd better get some fresh air in your lungs before you go," said Grandad. "Tha'll get none in Widnes."

21
"OUI, MONSIEUR"

By the time Alan arrived home it was nearly ten. The house was empty. His mum had probably gone to town. He had a couple of hours to kill before he went out again. He was meeting all the lads at half past twelve at the bus station. He went upstairs and flopped onto his bed. He was still suffering from the effects of the previous night; four pints in the pub, a couple more in the Floral Hall and then those rum and blacks. He closed his eyes for a couple of minutes zzzzzzzzzzz...!

By the time he woke up, Alex Murphy, Bob Dagnall, Dick Huddart, Ray French and the rest of the Saints team were tying their bootlaces, applying the last dollops of vaseline to their faces and legs and listening to the final words of wisdom from coach Stan McCormick.It was nearly half past one. He couldn't believe it. He wondered if he was still dreaming.

"I thought you were going to the match," said his mum, as he staggered into the kitchen.

"So did I. Why didn't you wake me?"

"I've only just walked in. I called in at Silkstone Street and finished up staying for my lunch."

When he walked into Granny's living room after tea, Uncle Stanley was in there.

"Hello Alan, a good win today eh? I thought Brian McGinn had a belting game."

They all laughed when they heard what had happened.

Later on he and Thelma walked into The Globe. Dorothy, Ronnie, Jenny, Ken, Sylvia and Geoff were already there along with an old friend, Johnny Shufflebottom, and his wife Margaret.

"Where did you get to this afternoon?" asked Ronnie before he had even sat down. "Don't tell me you didn't wake up?"

"Do you know, he's always been the same," said Dorothy. "He was just like it when he was at school. He's the only person I know who can go to sleep standing up."

"Do you remember that time we were stood in assembly?" said Ronnie. "He was right at the end of the line. After prayers we all filed out and he was left there on his own, fast asleep."

To avoid any further embarrassment he offered to get the next round in. While he was at the bar Geoff said, "Did you hear that tale about him when he fell asleep in the work's surgery?" He went on, "He'd cut his arm when he was shinning up a pole at the back of the Foundry. So he shoots down to the surgery and one of the nurses bandages him up. She told him to go and have a lie down in the side room. Shortly after, she went home, it was nearly finishing time, and then the other nurse, not knowing he was in there, locked the door. He never heard her. He nodded off straight away. By the time he woke up there was nobody there and he had to ring the gatehouse to get out."

By the time he returned with the drinks, they had started talking about the summer holidays.

"Where are you two going this year?" he heard Ken ask John and Margaret.

"We're going back to France. We had a great time last year."

"The only bad thing was we couldn't speak the lingo," said Margaret."I wish we'd gone to night school."

"Maybe Alan could give us a few lessons before we go. He can speak French, he keeps telling us."

"Ah oui, d'accord, ca sera tres interessante, je peux commencer immediatement, si vous voulez?"

"You shouldn't have asked him, John," said Ken. "You've started him off. He'll only get worse."

Ignoring his comments, and to demonstrate his linguistic skills, he launched forth, throwing his arms out and knocking an ash tray over Thelma and a bottle of Babycham over Sylvia.

"Who let him know we were coming here?" said Ronnie. "I thought we'd come for a quiet drink after last night."

"They are making a film about Greeno, you know?" said Geoff, "Billy Liar it's called. The fantasy world of an imbecile."

The banter carried on until they were interrupted by the arrival of a Salvation Army woman selling the War Cry.

When she had gone, Sylvia said: "I can't stand them lot coming round the pub, when you're all having a good time. Why can't they knock on your door like everybody else does?"

"Eh, I can't stand any of them knocking on our front door," said Jenny. "We had the Jehovah's Witnesses round last week. I couldn't get shut of them. By the time they'd gone, my tea had gone cold. A lovely bit of black pudding it was."

"You wouldn't have objected to Alan knocking on your door with his petition would you? You wouldn't lump him with all the religious freaks, would you?"

"Oh no. Just the normal freaks."

"He must have knocked on every door in Ashurst," commented Geoff.

128

"He was knocking on doors at all times of day and night," said Dorothy. "I heard that he was knocking on Ivy Marsden's door at midnight."

"And that was to get out," laughed Ken.

It went on like this all evening. They were still at it as they tried to get into the town's newest eating house. In addition to forty seven chip shops and two Italian coffee bars, Ashurst now boasted a Chinese restaurant, The Golden Moon in Standish Street. But as was usually the case on a Saturday night, it was full so they decided not to bother.

As they walked home Alan said, "Well, do you like my little coterie of chums. Do you find their company intellectually stimulating and spiritually uplifting?"

"If you mean, did I enjoy myself tonight the answer is yes, but I couldn't face any more beer for a bit."

"So where do you fancy going tomorrow night?"

"Can we go to the Rivoli? East of Eden's on."

Unfortunately she had got it wrong. The James Dean film began on Monday and ran for the rest of the week. The show they saw began with Laurel and Hardy, followed by a documentary about Whitley Bay. After the Pearl and Dean adverts, they had to endure 'The Hero from Sand City', a third rate western made worse by the fact that the sound was out of synchronisation.

Until she had watched the film about Whitley Bay, Thelma had not thought about the summer holidays. But during the main film, as her mind began to wander, she had begun to think of all the places she would like to visit. Turner's ran coach trips all over the place, Fleetwood, Blackpool, Windermere, Llandudno, the Peak District. They could also catch the train and go to Southport or over to the Wirral, and she fancied a day out in Liverpool just walking round. As they walked home it seemed as good a time as any to raise the subject.

"Whitley Bay looked quite a nice place. Have you ever been there, Alan?"

"No. I've never been up Geordie Land."

They walked along for a bit and then she asked: "Alan, what are you doing about your holidays this year?"

She fully expected him to say, "I don't know. Why, what do you fancy doing?" But his answer completely shocked her.

"I'm going hitch hiking in France."

They had just reached the house as he spoke, and as they walked up the steps to the front door, she quietly said: "Well, I hope you'll send little me a nice postcard."

She went straight into the kitchen to make a cup of cocoa, like she always did. While the milk was boiling, she began to mull over what he had said. It had upset her. She was sure they were going to spend a lot of the holidays together. She thought everything was going well between them and suddenly this.

Perhaps she had misjudged him, perhaps he had only kept going out with her because of the way things had developed since Christmas Day. If she hadn't been living at his Granny's, maybe it would have been different. Perhaps the situation she had found herself in had contributed to a great misunderstanding and now she was going to face the reality of it all.

She trudged back into the living room with the cups in her hands. The great love of her life ignored her as she sat quietly beside him. He was avidly reading the same Football Pink he had done on Saturday night. After what seemed an age she asked: "Which part of France are you going to, Alan".

"I don't know," he replied without taking his eyes off the paper. "I haven't decided yet."

Ever since she had moved in with Auntie Lil she had had a cup of cocoa last thing at night. While she was drinking, she would usually be reading as well. But when she didn't feel like reading, usually when something had gone wrong in the day, when somebody had upset her or let her down, she would sadly watch the cocoa bubbles. But she hadn't done that since before Christmas, not until tonight when it seemed like all the good times were coming to an end.

She waited a few more minutes and then muttered: "Who are you going with, Alan?"

He put down the paper and lifted up her chin. He saw once again that sad little face, just like that time in Marios when she had told him she had nowhere to go on Christmas Day. And when he saw the tears in her eyes and on her cheeks he realised his little joke had misfired. She had taken him so seriously. She hadn't realised he was just having her on.

"You, you barmpot. Who else do you think I would want to go with?"

She threw her arms around him and gripped him tightly.

"I thought you were wanting to go on your own or with somebody else. I thought you were getting fed up with me. I thought, I thought you didn't want me any more."

She sobbed as she spoke. He could feel her heart bumping against his chest. He was annoyed with himself. He shouldn't have misled her like that. He wished he had just asked her straight if she would like to go on holiday with him and then watch her face when he said France. He ran his hands up and down her back and across her shoulders, and after what seemed an age, she slowly let go of him and said:

"You're not just going out with me because you feel sorry for me, are you Alan?"

He looked closely at her as she spoke, just like on Christmas Eve. So much had happened to her since then, all for the better he thought. But she obviously still felt a little insecure, perhaps the scars from her childhood were taking longer to heal than he

130

realised. Or maybe now it was simply a case that she didn't want to lose him.

"Look Thelma, let me be totally honest with you. I always have been, but I think sometimes you don't know when I'm having you on. Yes, I did feel sorry for you when I heard you'd nowhere to go over Christmas, and when you told me you'd been brought up in a home. But that's all in the past now. You see, well maybe I don't always express what I feel too well. Sometimes I don't quite say what I mean, but I'll just say this like they do in France. I'm sure of it now, you see Thelma, je t'aime."

She wrapped her arms round him again.

"Well, let me tell you something Alan Greenall, I je t'aime you as well."

She continued to cry for a while but she was smiling at the same time. After a few minutes she sat back, wiped her eyes and her cheeks, took hold of his hands and said

"So you really want to take little me for a holiday, do you? What ever have I done to deserve that?"

"Yes, I do. Do you want to come?"

"Oui monsieur."

"And if you behave yourself while we're over there, I'll think about bringing you back as well."

"So where are we going, and where will we stay?"

"Why don't you come up to our house on Tuesday night after work? I'll get the maps out and show you the route."

"Oui monsieur."

It was turned twelve o clock before he finally left. Thelma washed and wiped the two cups, tidied up the settee, turned out the lights and as she walked up the stairs, she saw Grandad coming out of the bathroom.

"Hello, love. You're up late. Are you alright."

And much to his suprise and amazement, she happily replied:

"Oui monsieur."

22
THELMA'S FIRST MATCH

As soon as he walked into work, Harry Groves came straight out of his office to see him. "Alan, can you go to Cammell Lairds with Neil Birchall. They've rung up to say that junction box you drew won't fit and they want to run the cables tomorrow. I'm sure they're wrong, but you'd better go and check it. It shouldn't take long. You should be back this afternoon."

In case he wasn't, Alan asked Charlie if he would give Ronnie and Thelma a lift after work before he had to leave. On the way they called in at Napiers in Kirkby. "I'll only be a few minutes," Neil said. But his idea of a few minutes wasn't very accurate. By the time he returned, Alan was fast asleep on the grass in the warm morning sun.

They drove down towards the Mersey Tunnel but stopped again at Marsh Lane sub-station. "I've just got to drop a couple of relays off here. I'll only be a few minutes. And in case you're thinking of nodding off again I wouldn't if I were you. This is Bootle. Round here, even the bugs wear clogs."

By half past eleven they finally arrived at the shipyard. The job that Neil had come to do didn't take much time. Alan's task took him no time at all. Somebody else was wrong for a change. The junction box was there, bolted to the wall just like he had shown it on his drawing, and cabled up and terminated as well.

"I'd better ring Grovsy."

"O.K., but tell him you've got to help me this afternoon, if he asks what time you're coming back."

After they had eaten in the works canteen and were walking back to the car park, Neil said, "Right old lad, just one more call to make."

"Where to now?"

"New Brighton. I hope you've brought your cozzy!"

"You're joking."

"You wouldn't put money on it, would you?"

And so for the rest of the afternoon Wilkinson's paid two grown men to paddle in the sea, build a sand castle and fall asleep on the beach.

On the way back, Neil dropped Alan off at the top of Croppers Hill. When he arrived at Ronnie's auntie's, Dorothy was already there. She worked at Pilkington's Ravenhead works, which was within walking distance of Doulton street.

As she opened the door she exclaimed, "My God Alan, whatever have you done to your face? It's as red as a beetroot!"

"Wash it with some milk with a drop of vinegar in it," Ronnie's auntie said. "That'll take the sting out of it."

But it wasn't the sting he was too bothered about. He knew he would have quite a bit of explaining to do when he got back to work in the morning.

As soon as Thelma and Ronnie arrived, Alan offered to go to the chip shop.

"I'm starving, I've had a very busy day."

Ronnie's auntie gave him four plates and a jam jar. As they walked down the street, Thelma said, "Why are you taking them?"

"The jar is for the mushy peas, and you'll have to work it out for yourself what's going on the plates."

"Well, I've never seen that before. It must be another of your quaint old Lancashire customs."

There was a great pile of bread on the table when they returned. After they had finished, Ronnie's auntie brought in an enormous apple pie and then some scones. She always treated them as though they hadn't eaten for weeks.

They left the house at seven and walked up to the ground. As they crossed Dunriding Lane, they could see the long queues forming, but by twenty past they were through the turnstiles and heading for their regular spot on the half way line. Mogger was there already along with two of his mates from work.

"Have you been on your holidays, Greeno?" was the first thing he said. But before Alan could reply, Mogger went on to tell them that Vollenhoven wasn't playing again, so Johnson kept his place on the right wing. In addition Mooney was at centre in place of Williams and Goddard was playing instead of French. He always seemed to know the line up before anybody else. Perhaps it was something to do with him being a player.

Alan introduced Thelma to him. "Neil was at Lane Head school with us."

As soon as Thelma opened her mouth, Mogger asked her if she came from South Wales.

"I thought so," he said when she nodded. "You sound just like my auntie Jenny."

"It's her first game."

"Well, I hope you like it. I wish our Clare would come with us. She isn't interested."

"How's married life? I've not seen you since you got wed."

"Great. The novelty hasn't worn off yet."

"How long have you been married?" asked Thelma.

"Three weeks!"

"Where are you living?"

"We've bought a house opposite Peasley Cross Hospital. You'll have to come round and inspect it some time."

"Why? Does it need re-wiring?"

"No, you bugger.It's all been done up. But don't come after half eight?"

"Why?"

"That's when we go to bed."

Then he turned to Thelma and said, "We've got one of your lot at full back."

"What do you mean?"

"He's on about our ace goal kicker, Kel Coslett. He's from Aberavon."

"Really."

"Eh, he's not the first Taffy we've had up here love. There's been some good ones over the years. But none of them could kick goals like he can."

This led on to another "Do you remember?" session. It was not the first time she had heard them talking about players, games and incidents from the past. They were always doing it. They talked about great tries they had seen, their favourites score and opponents who had been flattened. They talked about other grounds they had been to and social events that had occurred at the time. She noticed how the weather always seemed to play a big part in their reminiscences. No matter what time of year it was when they went to some grounds, it always seemed to be snowing, raining or blowing a gale. And nearly every time, there was a funny side to their tales.

She heard the names of George Parsons, Ray Cale, Reg Blakemore, Don Gullick and Glyn Moses mentioned. To her they were just names. But one thing she had in common with them was that they were all Welsh. And in a strange way she felt a great affinity with them.

As she listened to them talk she looked around at the people on the terraces. Some were stood there looking into space, others were in animated conversation. A few were still eating their evening meal, usually in the shape of a large pie out of a paper bag. There was a real buzz around the place. She felt good to be there in such a large crowd. She couldn't wait for it to start so she could see what it was really like.

Suddenly the crowd at the Eccleston end began cheering as thirteen players wearing red and white hooped shirts and blue shorts ran out of the tunnel and onto the field. She turned to Dorothy and screamed: "What a noise!"

"That's nothing. You wait till the Saints come out!"

"I thought that was the Saints. They do play in red and white, don't they?"

"Not tonight. They'll be in blue shirts. The home team has to change when the colours clash."

And then, just as she had said, there was a deafening roar as the St. Helens team ran on to the pitch. By now the ground was pretty full. Oldham had brought a large number of supporters and a large group of them were stood close by. Among them was one loud-mouthed individual, a right bag of wind he was. As soon as the game kicked off, he began a continuous barrage of abuse at the St. Helens' players, the referee and the two touch judges. And as he shouted out, he kept bumping into Thelma.

After a few minutes, another of the Oldham supporters pushed him back, leaned forward to her and said:

"You're all right love, he's harmless. He just gets excited. He's as bad as this when he goes fishing."

She kept quiet at first while she watched the early exchanges. As the game went on, Dorothy kept explaining to her what was happening and why the referee had blown his whistle or stopped play. Then, just before half time, the Saints Cumbrian forward, Dick Huddart, found a big gap in the Roughyed's defence and made a forty yard burst for the line chased by half the Oldham team. As he ran they heard her shouting, "Go on, go on, go on, go on", with the rest of them. And while she watched what was happening on the field she also heard all the banter from the people stood around them.

"Forward, miles forward, are you blind referee?"

"Stiff arm, that was deliberate, get him off, that's the third time he's done it!"

"Feeding, that went straight in the second row."

"Your glasses must be on the mantlepiece at home ref. You could see that from here."

"Gerrem onside, referee. Bloody Murphy's been offside all night."

"You call Watson a prop. I wouldn't let him prop clothes in our yard."

The banter went on and on. It was endless. Thelma thoroughly enjoyed it. By half time she knew she was going to enjoy watching the Saints.

As the teams were making their way back to the dressing rooms, Dorothy turned to her and said:

"Well, what do you think? Do you like it?"

"I do. It's great."

"Can you understand it all?"

"Well, not all of it."

"Like what?"

"Sometimes the referee gives a scrum when there's been a knock on or a forward pass, and sometimes he doesn't. Why?"

"Good question. There's no answer to it," said Ronnie. "It happens at every game you go to."

"It might be that he didn't see it from where he was stood at the time. Or then he might play advantage," said Alan.

"What's that?"

"If a Saints player knocks on and an Oldham player picks it straight up, the referee will let play carry on. It helps to keep the game flowing."

"Another thing I don't understand is when a team kicks the ball straight into touch. Sometimes the scrum is where the ball was kicked from, other times they don't have a scrum and they play the ball to themselves?"

So Dorothy briefly explained why. Then Alan asked if she had picked out her favourite player.

"I like number seven. He's so much smaller than all the others, and yet he's always in the thick of it."

"That's Wilf Smith," informed Ronnie. "He will be pleased to know he's got a fan now."

"Don't you knock him," said Alan. "He might not be as good as Murphy, but he's a real grafter. He'll do for me."

"Which one is Murphy?"

"Number six."

"Charlie's always on about him. Yes he's good as well, but I like the way Smith puts the ball in the scrum, then runs round to get it from the back."

They carried on talking, and then Thelma said: "I didn't think there'd be any fighting."

"Well it happens a bit. It's usually a heat of the moment thing. But don't worry, they'll all be the best of mates at the end," said Alan.

Mogger laughed. "You wouldn't say that if you'd played in the A team."

Soon the two teams reappeared and Thelma continued to watch avidly as the Saints stormed to victory, winning by twenty two points to eight. And the longer she watched the more she began to shout and cheer. A couple of times Dorothy turned to Alan, nodded at Thelma, and smiled. Alan remembered what she had been like on Christmas Day when they had been playing cards and all the noise she had made then. Sometimes she seemed like a big kid, but then as his Mum had said:

"Perhaps she's just making up for a childhood she never had."

As soon as the final whistle was blown, both sets of players shook hands and walked off the pitch together, chatting away just like old friends. Thelma was amazed at it all. She had just watched them knocking each other about; she had seen men thrown to the ground and dropped on; she had seen one of the Oldham forwards with blood streaming from a cut on his head, and late on in the second-half there had been a right old punch up. But as Alan said, when the game was over they were all the best of mates again. Amazing!

As they walked back into Dunriding Lane, they saw a great long queue for the buses so they decided to walk back into town. As they approached the end of Knowsley Road, Ronnie said to Thelma:

"What do you think of that beautiful building?"

Before she could reply he went on:

"That's my old school."

"Every time we come past here, he tells us that," said Alan.

"I thought you went to Lane Head?"

"I did, but we used to live round here until I was seven. This was the first school I ever went to."

And then, as he always did, he climbed up the wall and held on to the railings to see where Mrs. Foster used to read those magical stories about a flying pink elephant when he was only five years old.

Once they were back in Ashurst they decided to call in for a drink in The Junction.

"Alan can get the round in," said Dorothy, "he's bound to have made something out of his expenses today."

As he went to the bar, she turned to Thelma and said:

"What are you two doing about holidays this year? Are you going anywhere?"

Before Thelma could reply, Dorothy continued:

"You see my auntie has got this big farmhouse up near Carlisle. There's loads of room. How do you fancy coming up with us for a week? Ken and Jenny are coming as well."

"We've already made some plans."

"Don't tell me, Thelma. He's promised to take you trainspotting at Golbourne?" laughed Ronnie.

"Maybe they're going to watch the speedboat racing at Carr Mill," laughed Dorothy.

"They might even go as far as Southport," said Ronnie.

"No, it's further than that".

"Blackpool?"

"No, further."

"Wales?"

"No, further."

"Cornwall?"

"Further."

"You can't get much further in England?"

"Who said it's in England."

"Scotland?"

"No."

"Ireland?"

"No."

"The Isle of Man?"

"No."

"France?"

"Oui. La belle France."

"I bet he's taking you hitch-hiking. And you'll be eating frogs legs and snails. You'll finish up as puddled as he is."

At that point, Alan returned with the drinks on a tray. As he carefully put them down before them Dorothy said in a pronounced French accent:

"One for moi, one for heem and one for Madame Greenall."

23
CHARLIE'S OTHER SIDE

"You had some nice weather for your day off," remarked Yorky as Alan was removing the cover from his board.

"It wasn't a day off. I was working."

"Oh aye. You could've fooled me."

"I was. I went down to sort out that junction box."

"There were only twenty wires in the bloody thing. You can't tell me that took you all day."

"I had to help Neil Birchall after I'd finished what I had to do."

"You were probably helping him build a sand castle more like as not. I bet you spent most of the day at New Brighton."

"I tan easily. I got this at the match last night."

"Eh, Greeno, I was there as well, don't forget," said Charlie. "I never even saw the sun".

"It doesn't shine in the Edington Stand. It never has done."

They carried on having a go at him. Fortunately both Harry Groves and John Battesby were out so neither could see the evidence. Then, just as Joan came into the office with the tea trolley, Mick said:

"That's enough lads. Give the poor lad a break. One thing is for sure, he won't get a tan like that when he's in France. He'll be in bed most of the time."

"What do you mean?"

At this point Charlie started to sing 'Under the Bridges of Paris' and Dickie shouted out, "Don't forget to visit the chemists before you go."

"So I gather you've heard."

"Oh yes, we've all heard. They put it out on the tannoy."

"And what will you be telling your mum and Granny about the sleeping arrangements?" laughed Yorky.

"We'll be staying in Youth Hostels."

"Oh aye, and I'll be having a fortnight on a desert island with Brigitte Bardot," the Yorkshireman replied.

As soon as they had finished their morning tea break, Stan put on his coat.

"Are you going out again Stan?" asked Charlie.

"Yes."

"Don't forget to take some sun cream with you then."

"There'll be no need for that where I'm going."

"Why? Where are you off to?"

"Havanna."

"In Cuba !"

"No. At the bottom of Wigan Lane, you pillock."

Later on that morning there was only Alan and Charlie left in the office. Len was in a meeting with Mr. Williams and all the others were out in the factory.

"So when did you two decide on this holiday?"

"Sunday night, after we'd been to the pictures."

"I bet she was over the moon, wasn't she?"

"Well, not at first. I'm afraid I upset her."

"How?"

Alan told him what had happened.

"You dozy bugger. Whatever did you do that for?"

"It was only a joke. I thought she'd know I would want to take her with me."

"She obviously didn't."

"I won't mess her around again."

"I hope you don't. Look Alan, she's a smashing kid, but you've still got to be careful with her. You don't know what's still going on in her head. She's only been living at your Granny's six months at the most, hasn't she? Before that she hardly had the best of it, did she?"

"No."

"I know they do what they can for them in these homes. But it can't be like having your own mum to look after you, can it."

"No."

"Just think of it, Alan. When she was a little kiddie, who would have read her endless bedtime stories and held her hand for hours until she dropped off to sleep. Did anyone keep stroking her brow when she was poorly? Or tell her it didn't matter if she pee'd in the bed? Whoever gave her a big cuddle when something went wrong, or simply because she was who she was? I bet deep down, she still feels a bit insecure, despite all your Granny and Grandad have done for her."

"Eh, I've never heard you talk like that before, Charlie. You're a big softy after all."

"Well, there's nothing wrong with that. This world's a tough enough place as it is. I know your dad got killed in the war, but you always had your mum there and your big brother and sister and all your relatives nearby. Poor Thelma, she didn't have one relative. Not one relative, Alan, all the time she was growing up."

140

"I know."

"And I'll tell you something else. If I'd known about her before Christmas, she could've come and lived at our house if she'd wanted to."

"Eh, you've a heart of gold. You'll get into Heaven yet."

"You hypocrite. You keep telling us all you're an atheist. You don't believe in Heaven."

"Well, maybe I believe in angels. After all I'm going out with one."

"Very funny, but listen, let me just say a couple of other things to you, while there's no one else about. I don't know but you might be the first lad she's ever been with. On this holiday, well she might say yes just to please you when really she means no. Don't make her do anything she doesn't want to do, or anything she isn't ready for. I know I'm no shining example of good behaviour when it comes to women, but I'm sure you know what I'm getting at."

Alan said nothing but smiled to himself. He knew about some of the scrapes Charlie had got himself into over the years, both before and after he was married.

"And another thing. If what happens happens, make sure you take some precautions. You don't want to put her in the club do you?"

Alan listened carefully. Charlie was old enough to be his dad. Sometimes he almost acted as though he was. He would often describe himself as a simple working class lad from St. Helens. Simple he wasn't, working class he certainly was, and proud of it. If only the world was made up of a few more people like him, it would be a far better place in which to live.

Alan knew he would not be the first lad Thelma had ever been with, but he said nothing. That was not for any of them to know anything about. He now knew about her background, maybe not everything, but enough. He knew about some of the things that had happened to her after she had left the home and was at the soap works. That was a time when she had been hoping to get a lot more out of life than she had had so far, but didn't. After that she had gone to work in Rhyl. That was a place where many short-lived romances developed, where young men went for easy conquests and promised to keep in touch after the holidays were over, and never did. Thelma had survived that experience, but she was luckier than some of the girls who went home at the end of the summer with much more in their stomachs than they had started with.

"What does she do in the evenings?"

"She talks to Granny for hours on end. She watches television, and she still reads a lot as well."

"Does she go out much?"

"Yes. She goes up to see her friend Beryl up Nook End every week and my Auntie

Doris and Uncle Jack and play with his tropical fish."

"How can you play with fish?"

"Well, you know what I mean, look at them."

"What did she think about Monday night?"

"She really enjoyed it. You should have heard her shouting and cheering. She's going to start watching them regular."

"Did she follow it all?"

"I think she did, most of it. Dorothy was very good with her. She kept telling her what was going on."

"And what did she think about my mate Alex?"

"All right. But she took a right fancy to Wilf Smith."

"I thought he had a good game. I don't know why folk knock him so much. He made the first two tries and you couldn't fault his defence."

The way Charlie had talked over the last half hour or so was so different than the way he usually did. But he soon reverted back to his usual self as the door burst open and in walked Dickie followed closely by Yorky.

"Hey, what are you two up to stood in that corner? What are you plotting now?"

"We're just discussing what to buy you for your birthday."

"Ha, Ha."

They were soon joined by Mick, who had been in the foundry. He flopped down on his stool, and as he began to pull off his boots he asked Alan:

"What's wrong with Thelma?"

"Nothing. Why?"

"I've just been talking to Tony Cropper and he reckons there's something wrong with her. He reckons it might be brain damage."

"Mick, what's up, what's happened to her?"

"Don't you know? Haven't you heard? She's started watching the Saints. She must be easily entertained. I thought she had a bit more about her."

"You're a typical Wiganer," said Charlie. "What do you lot know about brain damage? You don't have any brains!"

But before any more could be said, Len and Ray Hewitt came back from their meeting with Mr. Williams.

"There'll be a meeting of the members in the Horse straight after work."

"Why? What's up Len? I were going into town," said Yorky.

"They're trying to sack Henry from the Lab."

"Why? He's been there for years."

"He's told them he won't work on that job for South Africa; that railway job. As far as he's concerned it's a matter of principle, and it's against the union policy."

142

"Why has this happened now?" asked Stan. "They never asked Henry to do that work before."

"Well, Oberfuehrer Wood is the boss man now. He's just trying to get his own back for that work to rule we had."

"If we let Lurch get away with this, we might as well pack it all in now," said Charlie.

"Too true. I think I'll ring up Ken Glover and see what he suggests we do. No doubt he'll have some good advice for us."

The afternoon shot by as they all discussed the issue. It looked like being a pretty heated meeting. Already there were mutterings of resignations if it came to a strike.

By ten past five they were in the back room of the Horse and Jockey. Len began by telling them he had rung the Divisional Organiser, reported back to the Office Committee what he had said and, after some discussion, he and Ray had gone to see Mr. Williams.

"Why didn't you tell the rest of us what Glover said first?" shouted out George Pennington. "It's supposed to be us that makes the decisions. That's what you told us when we all joined this union."

"Pipe down," said Dickie loudly. "What do you think he's doing now? Let him finish."

"Well, if it comes to striking, I'm going to drop out." It was, not suprisingly, Ernie Broadbent.

"We won't miss you." Dickie quickly said.

"If you two shut up, I'll give you the full story and then you'll really have something to get upset about."

It sounded ominous.

"I came straight to the point. I told him he shouldn't expect us to sit back and do nothing if he sacks Henry. We made it clear he would have a dispute on his hands."

"You can't say that, not without asking the members first. Some of us might not agree with the Office Committee. And what has South Africa has got to do with us. It's political."

Len let Harry speak, ignored what he said and carried on.

"I asked Williams whether he thought it was worth it for the company to get itself into this situation, just because some jumped up little Hitler had let his new found power go to his head. Henry has worked in the lab for over fifteen years. Lurch hasn't been there for more than ten minutes. Then I told him what he was like when he worked in the Drawing Office and how much better things were since he left. And I finished up by telling him it wouldn't be in his interests or ours if we started missing deadlines just because of one pig-headed individual."

"I wish I'd never joined this union," said Ernie.

"So do we," said Dickie.

"Shut up you two. You're like a pair of old washer women. I know what's worrying Williams. It's that Kowloon job. If there's the slightest delay now, it won't be on the docks by Tuesday and there's a big penalty clause on it."

"But we've all finished on that job weeks ago," said Frank Hodgson. "Don't tell me you are going to involve the shop floor as well, because if you do, every time they have a dispute they'll be wanting us to come out with them. My God, this thing is going to get out of control."

"We're not asking them directly, although they probably would help. The thing is the assembly shop fitters can't work without supervision. If the foremen came to our meeting straight after work, they will all get sent home, and I know the inspectors were being asked to stay until midnight to get the job passed off."

"Anyway, at this point Williams asks for an adjournment. Half an hour later he calls us back in. He told us he didn't want a dispute over the matter. As far as he was concerned he would drop the whole matter on three conditions."

"What are they?"

"Let him finish, Ernie."

"One, we would call off tonight's meeting. Two, there would be no further action on the matter and three, we would accept that the management has the complete right to manage the place."

"I hope you agreed to it," said George Pennington.

"Well if he had, we wouldn't be in this meeting would we, you daft bat," commented Dickie.

Len smiled and went on.

"I told Williams I couldn't cancel the meeting otherwise the members would complain that the Office Committee never keep them informed. However, I was prepared to excuse any of our members from this meeting who had been asked to work overtime tonight. I made no reference to us accepting their right to manage."

"Half of them couldn't manage a hot dinner," laughed Yorky, "or get here on time."

"So does that mean Henry keeps his job?" asked Stan. "It seems a bit too easy."

"Has anything been said to you, Henry?" Ray asked.

"Not yet, but Lurch got called away to the General Offices about four o'clock and hadn't come back by the time we all finished work."

"He's probably gone for a bollocking."

"Well, knowing what he's like, he won't forget this affair. He'll be after getting his own back, and you'll be on his black list now, Henry," laughed Les Fishwick.

"Join the club," said Keith Sanderson. "You'll be in good company. We're all on it, all the mechanical lads."

"I would like to move that we support the actions of Len and the Committee," proposed Mick, now keen to get away for his tea.

Quite a few shouted out "Seconded", and when the vote was taken it was almost unanimous. Only Ernie and George had abstained, for what reason no one knew or cared.

"I'd just like to say one other thing before I close the meeting. It is something I know you've all been looking forward to. There's a branch meeting next Thursday in the Boilermakers Club and there's a speaker from the Divisional Council coming. I'll send the details round tomorrow with the Vacancy List. And if there's no other business then I hereby declare this meeting closed."

24

I CAN KEEP A SECRET, IF YOU CAN

"Well, ladies, how did you enjoy your first union meeting?" asked Len.

"I nearly wet my knickers with all the excitement," said Rita.

"Listening to Dickie express himself to the Jig and Tool lot was worth the admission money on it's own," laughed Joan.

"What about you, Thelma? What did you make of it?"

"I was overwhelmed by it all, Len. I had to close my eyes when they were counting the votes. The tension was just too much for me."

Len smiled, then turned to Henry who had just bought them all a drink and said:

"Well, I suppose you'll be pleased with the outcome?"

"Not very."

"Why?"

"I've been in the union all these years. Suddenly I get my one big chance to become famous. Henry Mather, the one who started the great struggle of the British working class against apartheid. And what happens? It's all over before it's even started."

"Thanks a lot. I knew you would appreciate the great sacrifice we made for you."

"I bet we don't even get a mention in the Ashurst Reporter."

"I'll tell you what I will do. I'll send a report to the Union Editor. He can put it in the DATA journal."

"I know what we can do as well," said Yorky. "We can make Henry the office delegate to the next branch meeting. He can go and tell them all about it."

"Gee. Thanks a bundle, but you'll have to do better than that. I already go every month. It's a pity a few more of you don't come."

"I suppose I'd better start going now that we're getting organised. But I'm not going on my own," said Len. "How about you coming Charlie? You've always got plenty to say about what the union should be doing."

"It's no use me going. I don't speak Latin."

"Eh?"

"Well the last time I went it was when they used to have it at The Windmill in that little back room, when Joe Heywood was the secretary. There was only five of us there.

We must have spent the best part of an hour deciding whether we had a quorum. Well we didn't, so we finished up having an ad hoc meeting. It was ad hoc this and ad hoc that. I was bored summat rotten. I thought they were talking about fish!"

"Very funny. Well it's in the Boilermakers Club now. And it's a good pint in there too."

"What about some of you young ones coming? We could do with some fresh blood," said Henry.

"Don't go, Thelma," laughed Yorky. "You'll get put on the Women's Committee before the evening is out, and then they'll be wanting you to go to one of their weekend schools and you'll never be sane again."

"Eh, there's nothing wrong with them week end schools. I've been to a few in my time. You can have a really good weekend. It'll only cost you twelve and six and you stay at some very posh hotels."

"You're dead right, Len. Like at Morecambe in the middle of winter!"

Soon they were joined by two foremen, Billy Tunstall from the Rolling Mill and George Kilshaw from the Paint Shop. After a while Billy turned to Thelma and said:

"Did I see you outside Knowsley Road school last night?"

"Yes, we had been to the match."

"And how long have you been a Saints fan?"

"It was the first time I'd been."

"Did you like it?"

"Yes, it's great."

"What was that lad doing? Was he trying to climb over the railings?"

"It was my mate Harpo," said Alan. "He does it every time we walk past the place. It's his old school."

"Well you might be suprised to know I went there when we lived in Horace Steet. Happiest days of my life. I wish I was there again and knew what I know now."

"Don't we all."

Then, turning back to Thelma, Billy said "You've left it a bit late to start following the Saints. They've only got two more games."

"Aye, at home," interuppted Alan, "but they've got three away games."

"True. Oldham, Halifax and Bramley."

"Where's Bramley?" asked Thelma.

"It's between Leeds and Bradford".

"I've never been to Yorkshire before."

"Well, just remember this love. There's only one good thing in Yorkshire and that's the road back into Lancashire."

And then, in complete contradiction to what he had just said, he went on:

"By gum, I've had some good times over there."

"You worked in Yorkshire after you came out of the forces, didn't you?" asked George.

"Yes. I lived in Dewsbury nearly two years. I built Thornhill Power Station."

"What! On your own?"

"I might be good but I'm not that good. No. I had an apprentice with me."

"And what brought you back to civilisation?"

"The train! I was there all during that big freeze in 1947. I've never known anything like it. The only time I could ever get warm was when the landlady's husband was working nights."

"You tell a good tale Billy."

"Well, I've seen a few things in my time. And with me being the charismatic person I am, I just like to share them with lesser mortals like yourselves."

"I suppose part of your charisma is related to all those fascinating places you've lived in," laughed Charlie. "Parr, Haydock, Ashurst and now Leigh, the cultural centre of the Western world."

"Talking of culture, you've missed out the best place I ever lived in."

"Where was that?"

"Paris."

"Paris! How long did you live there for?"

"A week."

"A week! Is that all?"

"It might've only been seven days and seven nights, but I learned more then than some folk learn in a lifetime. And I don't mean going round museums and art galleries."

"When was that Billy?"

"June 1945. It was after we'd been in Germany. Did I never tell you about the time we fought our way across the Rhineland?"

"Many times," murmured Len.

Billy then turned to Alan and remarked: "That's when I won the George Cross."

Alan knew Billy had served all during the war, and had seen plenty action, but he was pretty sure the George Cross was not among the medals he had won. But before he could say anything Len said:

"Tell us that tale about when you were in that farmhouse near Duisburg and you met those two twins from Ashton."

"That always makes you laugh, doesn't it? But I can't. I've got to go," then looking at his watch he went on, "I'll just nip back into work and clock off."

"You mean you've been paid for sitting here drinking?"

148

"Greeno, you never change, do you? As gullible as ever. Well, I'm going. See you in Casablanca."

As he walked away, Alan asked:

"Why does he always say that when he leaves you?"

"Why does he say a lot of things?" Yorky answered. "He's a great bloke, but I sometimes think he's got a screw loose somewhere. You'd never think his dad was a University professor and his mother a ballet dancer."

"Were they?"

They all burst out laughing.

"You know, Greeno, it's you that's got a screw loose. You don't really think his dad was a professor, do you? You've obviously never seen him."

"Eh, Charlie, just because he looks like Groucho Marx on a windy day, doesn't mean he's crazy," said Len. "Appearances can be very deceptive."

"That's right," said Yorky. "He was no slouch, his old fellow. There wasn't much he didn't know about the production of transparent liquid containers."

"You mean he used to be a bottle hand."

"Very good, Greeno. You soon worked that one out." Then, turning to Thelma, Charlie said:

"Are they all as daft as him in their family?"

"I think you're all wrong about him. You just don't recognise genius when it's staring you in the face. It was just the same with Albert Einstein when he was a young man."

"Well, that's the first time I've ever heard anyone compare Greeno with Einstein. We must be missing something."

"I bet you didn't know that when his Grandad was a young man he was involved in the extraction of subterranean fossil fuel."

"Very good, Thelma. You certainly have a way with words."

"You'd better translate that for me, Charlie," said Yorky.

"It's her clever way of telling us that Grandad was a collier. I think that calls for a drink. What do you want Thelma?"

"Lager and lime please, Charlie."

"Anybody else want one?"

They all did.

As Charlie went up to the bar, Yorky said:

"What will Granny say if she finds out you've been sat in a pub drinking beer with a load of strange men?"

"Speak for yourself," said Len.

"And won't she be expecting you in for your tea?"

"No, she knows I'll be out for the evening. I've been invited to one of those stately homes up Chisnall Avenue."

"He's not asked you to go and look at his etchings, has he?"

"No," butted in Alan, "we're just getting our holiday organised."

"You're not really going to go away with him, are you Thelma?"

"Yes."

"I hope you like trainspotting. That's what he did the last time he went there."

The banter carried on for a while and then Charlie said, "Right I'm off, I've just remembered, there's a big match on tonight."

"Who's playing? You never said anything about it today."

"Thatto Heath Labour club versus Griffin Inn. There'll be a big crowd."

It was crown green bowls, Charlie's summer pastime. And no doubt tomorrow morning the Electrical section would hear all the details of this great sporting event, one that would attract the attention of at least a dozen passers by.

"And if you two are ready, you can have a lift. It'll be one and six to the roundabout, two bob if you want dropping off outside the house."

As they walked down Parry Lane, Alan asked Thelma:

"Well, what do you think of Billy Tunstall then?"

"He's hilarious. I could've listened to him all night."

"He's a great bloke. He's daft as a brush sometimes. You would never think he was a senior foreman. He's almost as daft as Mad Mick."

"Who's that?"

"Mick Ellison, one of his chargehands. Now he is mad."

A car drove past them, the driver pipped his horn and waved.

"Who was that?"

"Jack Large. He'll have been up to see his mother. She just lives at the back of us. Now he's another character."

"He always seems very dour when I've seen him at work."

"Oh, he never laughs does Jack, but he's one of the funniest guys I've ever met. He can have you in stitches and yet to look at him when he's talking, you'd think he was having a heart attack. You should hear him when he starts on about when he worked at the BI."

"What's that?"

"BICC. It's the cable works at Prescot. It stands for the British Insulated Callenders Cables. Jack reckons a truer description would be the Biggest Individual Collection of Comedians."

"I thought that was Wilkinson's?"

"Well they're probably both in the same league."

150

His Mum was sat watching Z Cars when they walked into the house.

"Hello Thelma, how are you?" Then she turned to her son and said: "Why are you so late, Alan? I thought you were coming home straight from work."

"There's been a big union meeting. They're organising a General Strike for next Thursday."

"Oh, not next Thursday. Your Uncle Norman is coming round. Why can't they have it at the weekend when folk don't have to go to work?" And she shook her head and smiled at Thelma.

"Anyway, go and sit down and I'll bring your tea in. It's been in the oven all this time. I hope it's not dried up."

She put the plates on the table, sat down besides them and said:

"I hear you're going to France, Thelma. Aren't you a lucky girl?"

Thelma smiled and nodded.

"Have you ever been abroad before?"

"Only to England."

"Do you think there might be some room for me? The only foreign place I've ever been to is Abergele," and with that she ruffled Thelma's hair.

"And whereabouts are you going, Alan?"

"Brittany."

"You're not going hitch hiking, are you?"

"Why not. It's the best way to travel."

"Well you be careful, if you've got Thelma with you. You should go on the train or the bus. It'll be a lot safer."

"You obviously haven't seen any French drivers."

After they had eaten, he laid his Michelin map of France on the table and pointed out the route they might take. They would start at Calais or Boulogne, head down the N40 to Abbeville, on to Rouen where they would cross the Seine, then down to Alencon where they would pick up the N12 and head towards Dinan and St. Brieuc and then along the coast road through St. Quay Portrieux and Perros Guirec to the the naval port of Brest. After that they would head South to Quimper, on to Rennes, through Le Mans and back up to Rouen and Dieppe where they would catch the boat back to Newhaven.

"That's a long way to travel if you're only going for a fortnight?"

"Yes, but don't forget mum, there'll be two of us, so it won't be so far."

Then he folded the map the other way and with his finger proceeded to show them the routes of his last two holidays: the 1961 expedition that had taken him right down to San Sebastian just over the Spanish border and last year's trip when he had reached Perpignan.

He told them of some of the longest lifts he had had and also the time he had travelled with a baker whose brother was racing in the Tour de France. He told them of the time he had got stuck between two small villages late one evening and had finished up sleeping under a tree and been woken up by a cow. He recounted the tale of when he was in a bar in Albi listening to students singing revolutionary songs. And when they heard where he was from, they asked him to sing an English song and he had brought the house down with 'Lassie from Lancashire'.

He told them about some of the characters he had come across and some of the out of the way places he had stopped at, and some of the bars he had drunk in. He made it all sound very exciting, but then it had been, well some of it.

But he didn't tell them about some of the other exciting things that had occurred, like the time he had been heading south out of Orleans with an American GI named Steve and they had stopped for two Australian girls who they later spent the night with in their tent in a field at St. Aubin de Blaye.

And he most certainly did not tell them about Simone, a teacher from Lille who was driving down to Tarbes for her daughter's wedding. In many ways she was like all the other women schoolteachers he had ever known. But although most of them at one time or another had smacked his hand, none of them had ever held it or any other part of him like she did. And whenever they had told him he was a naughty boy, well they had usually shouted it out in front of the whole class, not like Simone who prefered to whisper it in his ear, in the quiet of the hotel bed they had shared on Bastille night.

Yes, of all the teachers he had ever had, Simone was without doubt the one he would remember most fondly. He had often wondered about her since they had said au revoir on the main square at Dax. Perhaps she might even be a grandmother by now.

"And where will you stay at night, Alan?"

Quickly he replied:

"Youth Hostels. There are loads in that area." Then, turning to Thelma he continued: "We'll have to get an application form for you to join and one for your passport as well."

As they walked back to Silkstone Street later that evening Thelma said:

"What are the youth hostels like? You never seemed to have stayed in very many?"

"They're alright, but it's a lot better staying in the bars in town."

"I've gathered that from some of your tales. And I bet there were a few more things that went on that you didn't tell us about."

He laughed.

"So, where will we stay then?"

"The bars are better; there's always something going on, but you know what my mum and Granny are like?"

"You mean that you didn't want them to think we might be staying in the same room."

He smiled and said, "Something like that."

She leaned over towards him and gently kissed him on his neck as she squeezed his hand. And then with a smile on her face she said:

"Well, I can keep a secret if you can."

25
CONVERSATIONS ON A TRAIN

"Hello, Greeno. Long time no see. Where've you been hiding?"

It was Keith Barton, stood in the queue waiting to buy a ticket for the excursion train to Bramley.

"Hello, Keith. How are you doing?"

"Me. Aw Reet."

"Are you still working at Vulcan?"

"Aye. Where are you now? Are you still at Wilkinson's?"

"Yes. I'm working in the drawing office."

"A posh job, eh?"

"Not bad."

"I didn't think I'd ever see you in here."

"Why not? I've hardly missed a match since I finished playing football."

"No. I mean having to buy your own ticket. I thought they would have let you travel free, after what you did for them?"

"Oh, you mean that petition. That's just what I thought."

"Did you sign it?"

"Course I did. I think I signed it four times, but don't tell anybody."

"How's your mam?"

"Not so good. Her rheumatism's bad. And she was very upset about your Auntie Kitty and Uncle Billy. Well, we all were."

"Aye. They were a good pair."

"They were an' all. They were good to us. We couldn't have asked for better neighbours."

"Who's living there now?"

"A bloke from Burtonwood. We hardly ever see him. He works at British Sidac on nights."

"Well remember me to your mam, won't you?"

"Why don't you come round some time? She'll be more than pleased to see you again."

By this time they had reached the front of the queue. A man bought tickets for Keith and the other two men he was with. As the four of them walked away he said:

"How's the wife and kids?"

"Who was that?" asked Thelma after Alan had bought their tickets.

"Keith Barton. I used to knock about with him when I was an apprentice. He lives next door to Auntie Kitty's old house."

"Yes, I gathered that but I didn't know you were married?"

"Trust Keith to spill the beans. I was hoping you wouldn't find out."

They walked onto the platform. Ronnie and Dorothy were already there. As they were talking, their train appeared in the distance. Alan watched as it slowly steamed towards them.

"It's a Pat."

"What's that?"

"A Patriot class engine. You can tell them by their wind shields and square chimney."

"Surely to goodness, you're not still spotting trains?" said Dorothy. "And here was me thinking you were beginning to grow up."

He ignored her comments and as the train came to a halt he looked first for its number on the front of the boiler, 45535, and then the nameplate over the wheels on which was written the name Sir Herbert Walker K.C.B.

"It's my lucky day. I haven't got this one."

As soon as they had sat down in an empty carriage, Dorothy said:

"What do you think about grown men who still go spotting trains, Thelma?"

"Well, I used to think it was a bit silly, but I'm beginning to appreciate its attraction."

"Oh, no. She's really coming under his evil influence," said Ronnie. "She'll be collecting bus tickets and playing stonies in their street next."

Their journey took them across Chat Moss, then through Patricroft, Eccles and Manchester Exchange and then over the Pennines, through places Thelma had only ever heard of: Rochdale, Todmorden, Mytholmroyd, where Yorky used to live, Sowerby Bridge and Halifax. For her it was a fascinating journey. The countryside was so different from the flat industrial landscape of South Lancashire that she had now come to regard as home. With a bit of imagination it was almost like a journey across the Alps, she thought.

It seemed no time at all before the train was pulling into Bramley station. A hundred doors opened simultaneously and a great army of Saint fans descended onto the platform and set off walking up to Barley Mow, the home of Bramley Rugby League club.

"Isn't it a small ground?" said Thelma as soon as they had found a place on the terraces.

"It is if you compare it to Knowsley Road, but if you think our ground is big you want to see Odsal."

"Where's that?"

Ronnie pointed with his finger across the pitch.

"About five miles over there. It's where Bradford Northern play. They can get over a hundred thousand in it."

"Maybe," said Dorothy, "but it's still a right tip."

The Saints had to win their last four matches if they were to have any chance of overtaking Swinton, the current League leaders. Bramley were clearly the easiest fixture and the men in red and white did not disappoint their huge army of fans, winning by twenty one points to nine.

On the journey back to Ashurst they were joined by Neil Morris and his brother-in-law Tony. They discussed the game in great detail, or rather they all listened while Mogger made his analysis of where and how Saints had won. It was amazing just how much he could remember. There had been a few changes to the team that had beaten Oldham. Mooney and French had replaced McGinn and Goddard. Smith was at stand off with Murphy moving across to scrum half. But the main change was on the right wing where Tom Van Vollenhoven was back after injury. Inevitably the discussion moved on to his try and general contribution to the Saints' victory.

"So what did you think of Voll, Thelma?" asked Dorothy.

"Great. He's almost as good as Wilf Smith."

They all laughed, and Alan said:

"Did you notice he was playing at stand off?"

"Yes. I saw that Murphy was putting the ball in the scrum."

"And which do you think is his best position?"

"Don't tease her Alan," interrupted Dorothy, who was increasingly assuming the role of her big sister.

After a while, Thelma asked: "Is it right they can get over a hundred thousand people into Bradford's ground? It must be an enormous place."

"It is." replied Tony. "I was there for that Halifax Warrington replay. I've never seen so many at a match."

"The weather is always miserable when you go to Odsal. I've never known a place so cold," said Ronnie.

"They reckon the Ice Age started there," laughed Alan.

"If you think Odsal is bad, you want to go to Batley's ground. It's still in the Ice Age, that place. There was a two inch layer of ice when we played there last season. And that was in the dressing room."

"They make me laugh at Batley. Do you know what the ground is called, Thelma?

156

Mount Pleasant. There's nothing pleasant about the place. And have you seen how it slopes. At least Odsal's flat."

"Dewsbury is just as bad. They call their ground Crown Flatts. The only thing that was flat there was the beer."

They chatted on and soon they had left Yorkshire behind them. Thelma just sat back and listened to them as they talked. She was beginning to realise that there was a lot more to Rugby League than just what happened on the pitch. There was all the humour and the joking on the terraces. There was the analysis of the game after it was over and who had played well and who hadn't. Then there was the talk about the games they had seen in the past, and the social events associated with them. And she loved being part of such a large group. She had felt really great, walking up from Bramley station to the ground with all the other Saints fans.

She decided that she would go and buy herself a red and white scarf. That would tell the world she was a Saints fan. But it was not only that, she was also a Rugby League fan. She knew about the great rivalry between St. Helens and Wigan fans. She knew also of a similar rivalry between Lancashire and Yorkshire fans. But at the same time in the Rugby League world there was also a great bond of friendship. It was hard to define, but she could already sense it and she wanted to be part of it. It made her feel good, and it showed in her face.

"What are you smiling at?" Dorothy asked.

"Nothing. Maybe it's just because we're back in Lancashire," Thelma replied, thinking quickly.

They all laughed and Ronnie said:

"I think we'll have to make you a honorary Lancastrian, but it'll cost you."

"Where do you come from, love?" asked Tony.

"She was brought up in South Wales, but she's been living here for ages," said Dorothy protectively.

"Have you noticed how she's started talking like us?" remarked Ronnie.

"Am I?"

"Yes. You've started saying have you not, and can you not, and putting like at the end of all your sentences. I've been listening to you."

"Well, I'll go to the top of our street."

There was a lull in the conversation and then Tony said:

"It always amazes me why they watch Rugby Union in Wales. I just can't understand why Rugby League has never taken off down there."

"So what's the difference between Rugby League and Rugby Union?"

"To put it very simply, Thelma, in Rugby League the players handle the ball, in Rugby Union the spectators do!"

"No. Be serious Neil. It's a fair question. You see, there's a lot of basic differences. Firstly, when you get tackled in League you're allowed to get up and play the ball back to one of your own team. In Union you're supposed to let go of the ball when you're tackled so that one of your team can pick it up. Secondly, in Union you can kick the ball straight into touch. In League it has to bounce once in the field of play. In Union they re-start play with those silly line outs-when all the forwards jump up in the air for the ball. In League, it re-starts with a scrum. Union teams have fifteen players, League have thirteen."

"The main difference, Thelma, is that in League the main idea is to run with the ball in your hands and pass it. In Union they prefer to make ground by kicking into touch. Rugby League is a much better game to watch, but it's a lot harder to play."

"Have you ever played Union, Neil?"

"Yes, when I was doing my national service. I learned the difference between the two the hard way."

"How come?"

"After I'd done my training at Catterick, I was sent to a camp in Somerset. The first day I was there this officer asks the group I was in if any of us played rugger. He must have been important because when I said I did, he just told our sergeant that he wanted me for the afternoon."

"Maybe he fancied you," laughed Ronnie.

Ignoring the crack Mogger continued:

"It turns out they were a man short for their annual grudge match against the local RAF team. They must have been playing about ten minutes by the time I'd got changed and on to the field. When I first saw them, they all seemed to be running round like headless chickens. The ref waves me on and within a minute or so I picked up a loose ball and started to run with it. I side-stepped round the first three, dead easy, and then somebody hauls me down from behind. I must have made about forty yards. So I went down with the ball and then all hell broke loose. There were boots everywhere. I shouted held but no one took any notice. Then I saw this little fat bastard with a stupid moustache. He just kicked out at me. So I got up and nutted him and the ref sent me off. I kept telling him I'd been tackled but he didn't want to know."

"They can do that in Union."

"I know now, but I didn't know then. And what made it worse was the bloke I laid out was a high ranking officer, with some fancy double barrelled name. I couldn't understand why he got away with kicking me."

"Did you get picked to play for them again?"

"No. A month later they transferred us to Germany. I decided I'd play soccer instead while I was over there. It was a bit safer."

"Who for? You or all the others?"

"Ha, ha. Anyway Greeno, how come you never did your National Service?"

"You didn't get called up while you were an apprentice, and when I came out of my time, they had changed it. As long as you kept passing your exams, they kept giving you a deferment. And by the time I'd done my HNC, they'd stopped it altogether."

"Lucky bugger."

"Well, from what I heard from Steve Halsall, you didn't have too bad a time of it over there."

"I brought some happiness to a few lucky fraulein."

They chatted on and then Ronnie said:

"I wish we still had the Top Four play off."

"What's that?"

"Well, you see Thelma, until last season there was just one division. There were too many teams in it for them all to play each other. So they had to have a play off at the end of the season. The top team was at home to the fourth and the second team was at home to the third, and then the two winners met in the Final."

"So who would've played who this season?"

"If my arithmetic is right, Swinton will finish top, Saints second, Widnes third and Castleford fourth. So Swinton would've been at home to Castleford and we would've played Widnes, and then in the final we would play Swinton."

"Don't be so sure, Ronnie. Remember last season. Wigan finished top, played Huddersfield at home and got beat. Huddersfield, who'd finished fourth went and beat Wakefield in the final at Odsal."

"I bet you don't know when they had the first ever Top Four play off?" asked Mogger.

"No, but I'm sure you are going to tell us."

"1907. Halifax beat Oldham. And I bet you can't guess who Oldham beat in the semi-final?"

"No."

"Runcorn."

"I'm really glad you told us that. I've been wanting to know that for months."

Then Ronnie chimed in. "Here's one for you, Mogger. Two teams from the same town met each other in the semi-final in 1926. Who were they? What was the score and who was the full back on the winning side?"

"Pass."

"St.Helens Recs beat St.Helens thirty three nil, and the full back was my great Uncle Billy."

"I thought you were going to say it was you. Anyway, here's one for you, clever Dick. It's about that very match. Which ground was it played at, how many spectators were there and what were their names?"

By now the train was passing through Rochdale station and this prompted Alan to ask Mogger when he was going to start playing again.

"The start of next season, I hope. Another two months and I reckon my shoulder will be all right again."

"Two months and no rugby, whatever are we going to do?" said Dorothy.

"Not quite. Don't forget it's the all singing, all dancing Wilkinson's works seven a side next week."

"Who have the Drawing Office drawn in the First Round, Alan?"

"We're at home against the Winding shop."

"What do you mean at home? All the games are played on the same pitch."

"We were the first team out of Billy Eccleston's trilby."

"Billy Eccleston!" exclaimed Tony. "Is he still there? I thought he'd retired years ago."

"No. He still keeps turning up and doing a bit. Not a lot. Do you know him?"

"I knew his eldest lad, Pete. I was at school with him. I remember when I first went to their house. I thought it was his grandfather."

"He hasn't changed a bit all the time I've been at Wilkinson's. Same stupid haircut, same boiler suit and definitely the same trilby."

It was not long before they were back in Ashurst. They walked from the station into town and called in the Nags Head for a drink while they decided what they were going to do for the rest of the evening.

Four pints later they had had enough and decided to go home. As soon as they walked into the house, Granny jumped up from watching the TV and began fussing.

"Whereever have you been Alan? Are you both alright? I was beginning to worry. It's nearly ten o clock."

"We've only been to Bramley. It's not the end of the world."

"Yes, I knew where you were going, but they are a bit funny over there, aren't they? You never know what might happen."

"Ee. They're not like us Lancashire folk," said Thelma loudly.

"You've been drinking again, young lady. Whatever will you be doing next?"

"I think I'll go and water the flowers."

As she banged her way up the stairs, Granny said:

"She's all right, isn't she Alan? She's not been mixing her drinks or anything has she?"

"No, she's just tired. It's been a long day for her."

160

"Well, you look after her. It's not that long ago that she was very poorly."

"Yes, I know. Don't worry. She's fine. You should hear her shouting. "

Then he slumped in the chair and said:

"Granny, could I ask a special favour?"

"I know what you're going to say . Can I have some bacon, scrambled eggs, fried tomatoes, baked beans, three rounds of toast and a big cup of tea?"

"How did you know that? You must be psychic."

"No, Alan. I'm your Granny."

26

THIS SPORTING LIFE

The first Wilkinson's seven a side competion had been held in 1945 as part of the town's Victory celebrations. It had been kept going ever since by the efforts of Billy Eccleston. Billy, a labourer in the Rolling Mill, had put his heart and soul into this self-appointed task and gave up much of his spare time and much more of the company's to it. He would often tell his somewhat suspicious wife that he was late home from work, even in the depths of winter, because there had been some important seven-a-side business to attend to. He also used the same excuse to explain to his foreman why he was away so much from where he was supposed to spend his working day.

How he had managed to get away with it over the years was all down to a chance remark that had been made by Joshua Wilkinson to a gathering of his managers back in 1950. With a smile on his face he had told them, in the course of his Christmas address, to pay as much attention to detail as that Mr.Eccleston did with his Rugby competition. In Billy's eyes that was proof enough that he had approval right from the top to devote as much time as he could to ensure the success of this great sporting event.

To be fair to him, it nearly always ran smoothly, although there had been a few hiccups over the years, the most memorable being in 1953. On that particular occasion the draw had been held in the works canteen. Billy had organised things so that he sat behind a small table on the platform with the rest of them in the main body of the hall. Stricken by delusions of grandeur, Ashursts's own Bill Fallowfield had even sent out invitations to the local papers.

He began by asking if they could hear him at the back, a rather ridiculous question since there were no more than a dozen people in the place, all sat on the front row. Then to start the proceedings he stood up and leaned over to bang the table with the seven pound hammer he had borrowed from one of the fitters and to which he had tied some coloured ribbon. The force with which he used it split the flimsy table in two. As it collapsed it slid over the edge of the platform and crashed onto the floor of the canteen, bringing Billy, his hammer, jug of water and all the numbered balls with him.

Unfortunately for Billy, the whole episode was captured for posterity by the one member of the Press present, a young journalist with a Brownie camera, who was on his first assignments for the Ashurst Reporter. Short of local news that week, the front page showed a picture of the incident, with the caption "Rugby Cup Draw Starts in Farce".

This year there had been no such problem. The draw had taken place in the snooker room of the Social Club. By now it had become a big social event. There were probably around a hundred people in the room drinking their pints as Billy, sounding every bit like Eddie Waring at his best, pulled the balls out of that battered old trilby. Sixteen teams had been entered and by half past five the details were ready for whichever of the local or national papers wanted to print them. And the following day notices went up all over the factory listing the details which were:

Iron Foundry	v	Machine Shop
Rolling Mill	v	Wages Department
Electricians	v	Brass Foundry
Drawing Office	v	Winding Shop
Refinery 'A' Shift	v	Plumbers
O.C.D.	v	Refinery 'B' Shift
Transport Dept.	v	Works Maintenance
General Office	v	Apprentices

The main item for discussion for the next few days was around who should be in the team. Ken Backhouse, who had once played for the famous St. Helens amateur team, Uno's Dabs, was made team manager, with Les Fishwick as his assistant. After much deliberation the names of the seven men who would represent the drawing office were finally announced, with Alan picked to play on the right wing.

To beat the Winding Shop, Ken had a very simple plan: "Run them off their feet. Kick and chase it. They're all old men, but don't let them know I ever said that." He certainly had a point. Whereas all the draughtsmen were in their early twenties, most of their opponents were in their thirties and their captain, the foreman, Gerry Higgins, was turned forty.

Their match was the first to be played. Quite a large crowd had turned up to watch the action and within a minute they had seen the first try. Straight from the kick off Keith Sanderson caught the ball, ran about twenty yards and then, just as he was about to be tackled, flicked it out to Alan, who had come running in from the wing. There was a great gap before him. He went right through it and raced forty yards to score under the posts. Three minutes later, John Meredith, from well inside his own half, kicked the ball towards the corner flag. Alan sprinted down the touchline, easily outpacing the opposition, and as the ball reached the line he was there to fall on it for an easy try.

By the end of the first half it was clear that their opponents were done for. During the interval, Ken introduced a new element to their game.

"I want you to imagine you're a typical French team on tour. Throw the ball about like they would. Let's entertain the crowd with a bit of garlic flair. But no kissing when you score or I'll have to smack your bottom."

Gerry Higgins caught the ball from the kick off and to avoid having to run with it, he booted it right down into the other half. Alan dashed back to collect it and then proceeded to side-step his way round four of the opposition and then outpace the others in a fifty-yard sprint to the line. It was all too easy and the Drawing Office ran out winners by thirty three points to nil.

The following day there was no living with him. He strutted round the place as though he had won the Lance Todd Trophy. And what made it even worse for the rest of them was when Janice, the new office girl, asked him for his autograph. But then Charlie put him back in his place when he said:

"You know Greeno, last night with them shorts on, you had the looks of a very famous Australian winger."

"Who's that then?"

"Brian Bevan!"

In the second round they were up against the Brass Foundry. Ken called his squad together at lunchtime to explain his plan.

"This lot won't be as easy to beat as the Winding Shop. You've got to remember one thing. What they may lack in respect of ball handling skills they will make up for by being physical. So the key to success and your own health and safety is to keep the ball moving and not get caught in possession."

Once again a good crowd had turned up to watch. This time their game was the last, so they stood on the touchline and saw the Iron Foundry, Works Maintenance and the Apprentices win through to the semi-finals. Then it was their turn. From the kick off the ball went straight to Keith. He did exactly the same as he had done in the first game, making about twenty yards and then flicking the ball out to Alan who had come in off his wing. But this time there was no gap. Joe Anderson, one of the chargehands, was waiting for him. Alan had the ball under his right arm. He remembered how Vollenhoven had scored his try at Bramley on Saturday. He ran towards the right, then slowed down, making Joe think he was going to side-step to the left. Just as Joe moved to tackle him, he accelerated to the right and handed Joe off with his left hand. Easy. Now there was only space between him and the try line, or so he thought. He straightened up, focused his eyes on the posts and completely failed to see a stiff arm coming in from the left. By the time he had come round it was half time and the game as a contest was over, the Brass Foundry finally winning by twenty eight points to nil.

After that it was back to the much safer pastime of watching Rugby rather than playing it. A visit to Thrum Hall, Halifax was followed by a home game against Hull Kingston Rovers, and finally the last match of the season away to Oldham on a Thursday night. As always the Works Social Club had organised a coach. As they were waiting for it outside the Aspinall Street gates, they were joined by Tony Potter, owner of the arm that had literally brought Alan down to earth. He was sporting an enormous black eye he had received in the big derby match between the Iron Foundry and the Brass Foundry in the semi-final.

"Hello, Tony. Did some bugger stiff arm you as well? "

"Aye, but he did it with his boot."

"Well, you certainly look the better for it."

"How about you? No brain damage, I take it."

"No chance of that. He's got no brains". It was Dave Crompton, a friend of Alan's from his time as an apprentice. "Do you know what your best position is, Greeno? Stand off. Standing off the field of play."

"Well at least I played, which is more than could be said for some folk."

The last game of the season was a bit of an anti-climax. By now Swinton had won the First Division and Saints were assured of second place. Oldham had finished bottom of the league and were soon to be relegated to the Second Division. After the game, which Saints won by twenty four points to nine, they walked back into Oldham town centre. The coach was due to leave at half past ten so they had a good hour to spend in the town. They soon found a decent looking pub and walked into the best room.

"Are these seats free, old lad?" said Alan to an old man sat drinking on his own.

"Yes, there's plenty room for you all. Are you from St. Helens?"

"Not quite. We're from Ashurst."

"Well, that's as near as makes no difference."

They sat down, organised their drinks and started talking about the game. After a few minutes the old man turned to Thelma and asked:

"Are you from Cardiff?"

"Yes. How did you know?"

"I could tell as soon as you started talking."

"Do you know Cardiff?"

"Yes. I was brought up there."

"How long have you been living in Oldham?" asked Ronnie.

"Since 1923!"

"You didn't come up here to play rugby, did you?"

The old man smiled.

"However did you guess? Is it my flat nose."

"Who did you play for?"

"I didn't. My young brother did. He played for Belle Vue for a bit. I only ever played at home."

"What, Union?"

"No, League."

"Who for?"

"Ebbw Vale."

"I didn't know there were any Welsh teams. When was that?"

The old man put down his glass on the table, moved up towards them and leaned forward as though he wanted to tell them something that he didn't want anyone else in the pub to hear. He gave the impression that he was glad to be in company for a change.

"It must've been about 1908. I was eighteen."

"Was there just one team in Wales?"

"No. That first season there must have been about half a dozen. Let's see, there was us," and he put his thumb up in the air, "Merthyr Tydfil," and he tapped his first finger, "Barry, Treherbert, Mid Rhondda and who was the other one? I can't remember. Oo, yes Aberdare."

"I've never heard of any of them."

"Well, it didn't last long. Aberdare, Treherbert, Barry and Mid-Rhondda must have only played for one season. Us and Merthyr, we went on a bit longer, but by the time the War started it was all finished."

"Why?"

"Travelling was bad, having to come so far up north for many of our matches. The other thing was the people who ran the Rugby Union. They used to put all sorts of obstacles in our way."

As he talked Alan looked at him closely. In appearance he reminded him of his Uncle Billy. Thin, little colour to his skin or hair on his head, wearing a faded suit with a waist coat and a pair of brightly polished black boots. But in the way he talked, he was much more like his Grandad with his ability to make the past come alive.

They listened with interest as he told them about some of the games he had played in and the grounds he had been to. He talked about players who they had never heard of, but who clearly had been stars in their days. And sadly he would also tell them of some of his former teammates who had been killed or maimed during the Great War.

"Do you want another drink?" asked Ronnie, pointing to his now near empty class.

"Yes, please. A pint of mixed would do very nicely, thank you."

As Ronnie went to the bar to get the next round in, Thelma asked:

"How do you like living among all these Lancashire hot pots?"

"After forty years I'm just about getting used to it."

"Have you got any family up here?"

"Oh, aye. There's the wife, three sons, two daughters and a dozen grandchildren. And I sometimes think they all live in our kitchen."

He stopped talking for a moment to pass the time of day with one of his neighbours who had just walked into the room. Then he turned back to Thelma and asked her how long had she been living up north.

"About a year."

"And where are all your folks? Are they up here as well?"

"No. There's only me."

"I see," he said, nodding sympathetically and possibly aware of what that might mean.

"I was born in Tonyrefail. Do you know it? I lived there before I went to Cardiff."

"Yes. Well, I used to. I suppose it's all changed now. We had an auntie lived there. We always used to go there in the summer when we were kids. Me and my two brothers."

"Do you know Rosemount Terrace?"

"I do. Why?"

"That's where I lived. At number nine."

"Well, that's a coincidence. That's where Auntie Polly lived."

"What? At number nine!"

"No. In Rosemount Terrace."

"What number?"

The old man stroked his chin as he thought. "I think it was number thirty."

"Is she still there?"

"Oh no, she died about twenty years ago. The war was still on. It was around the time of Normandy. I remember, I went to her funeral. I think the whole street turned out for her."

It suddenly struck Thelma that she may also have witnessed the event. The Normandy landings had been in June 1944, her Mum had died in September, three months later. They must have been living there then. Perhaps her mum had come out of the house to pay her respects to an old lady who had just died. Maybe she had been holding Thelma in her arms as the funeral hearse was driven past.

But before she could ask any more questions, they were interrupted by the arrival of two heavily built men. They stood menacingly close, as one said over Thelma's head

"Are you all right, dad?"

"Hello, Eric. Yes, I'm fine. I'm just telling my young friend here about your Auntie Polly". Then turning back to the others he went on. "This is my eldest lad come to see if I'm getting into any bother."

"Well, it wouldn't be the first time, would it?"

They all moved round a bit to let the two men in. Eric introduced his mate to them and said to Alan and Ronnie:

"To look at him, you wouldn't think he could knock a hole in a wet paper bag, would you?"

"Are appearances deceptive then? Does he get into trouble?" asked Alan.

"You may not believe this, but last week he put two young lads in hospital."

"Let me out. I'll just go and pay a visit."

While he was away Eric told them what had happened.

"It was here in this room. There were these three lads in here from Failsworth. They were looking for trouble. They've been in before. He was just sat there on his own and one of these lads starts flicking his cigarette ash over his boots. One thing led to another and then he told them if they couldn't behave to get out. So, of course they laughed at him and one of them called him an old Welsh get. Then the other flicked his fag end at him and it dropped into his beer. So he stood up and said, 'I'm going', and they started laughing at him again and then he went on, 'to teach you children a lesson'.

"And just as he said that he picked up his walking stick, lifted it in the air and brought it crashing down on this lad's hand. Then he whizzed it across and hit the other one straight in the face. The third disappeared quick."

"What happened then?"

"They called the police and an ambulance for these two lads. One of them had got three broken fingers and the other one was bruised all across his face where my Dad had hit him. And of course all the regulars in the place swore blind he was acting in self defence."

It was over ten minutes before the old man returned. They could see him talking to various people sat around the room.

"I felt really sorry for him at first. He looked so lonely all sat on his own," said Thelma.

Eric laughed. "You needn't worry love. He knows more folk in Oldham than anybody I know."

Half an hour later, it was time to go. They had really enjoyed listening to the old

168

man, and he had obviously enjoyed talking to them. They stood up, shook his hand and wished him all the best. Then Thelma went over and kissed him on the cheek.

"You've made a big hit there dad," laughed Eric. "I'm going to tell my mam about you."

As they walked back to the coach Alan said:

"You liked him, didn't you?"

"I did. He was really nice."

"He was a bit like Grandad."

"Yes. And Welsh too. Just like little me."

27

"THIS IS THE SIXTIES, STAN"

The first Monday in June saw the arrival of John Rigby, the new electrical draughtsman. For the first few days they didn't get much opportunity to talk to him. There was a big rush to complete all the outstanding jobs before the Works Shutdown. And Mr. Williams, along with John Barker, the Works Progress Manager, spent an enormous amount of time in John Battesby's office. As a result it was not until the Friday lunchtime session that they had a chance to find out about their new colleague.

"Did you work at the BI before?" asked Charlie as they sat down in the back room in the Hope and Anchor.

"Yes."

"What made you come here?"

"They're moving the section I was on to Kirkby. I didn't fancy going. And I could do with a change. I've been there since I was sixteen."

He told them a bit about the work he had been doing and then asked if it was always so busy and so quiet.

"You've chosen a funny time to start. It's always like this in the run up to the Works Fortnight. And the other thing is, the Managing Director rarely spends so much time anywhere near us."

"With all this work on, I thought we would've all been on overtime."

"We're in dispute with them. They won't pay for the first half hour and then they'll only pay flat rate, so we aren't working any."

"Have you found out if he's in the union, Len?"

"No problem Charlie. It was the first thing I asked him when I got the chance."

"How strong are they at the B.I.?"

"They're just getting DATA organised. Their problem is the company Staff Association. It negotiates the wages."

"We used to have one here," said Yorky. "Hopeless it was. All it does now is run dances."

"How does Ray describe their situation?" said Charlie. "Cast into the dustbin of history by the social pressure of economic forces, or something like that."

"Len is the C.M. here," laughed Mick, "but Comrade Hewitt is the real power behind the throne."

Len smiled, but said nothing for it was true. Ray was forever coming up with some clever plan, he always knew what wages were being paid at factories all over the place and he was well known for putting things in their correct historical context, or was it hysterical context.

They talked for a while and then Charlie asked John if he watched the Saints.

"No. I don't like blood sports."

"So who or what do you do in your spare time?"

"I'm in a band."

"What? Do you mean a brass band?"

"This is the sixties, Stan," laughed Charlie. "I bet he's in a rock and roll band."

"Like the Beatles."

"Yes."

"Oh, my giddy aunt."

At this point Tony started banging on the table and singing out, "Love, Love Me Do".

"Am I right, John?"

"Yes."

"What's it called?"

"The Rainmen."

"Why did you call it that?"

"Two of the band live in Rainhill and the drummer comes from Rainford."

"And where do you live?"

"Behind Prescot Cables football ground."

"How long have you been going?"

"Since Christmas."

"And where have you played?"

"All over the place. Last Friday we were at a farmers' ball in Ormskirk, Saturday at a wedding in Widnes and tonight we're at Parr and Hardshaw Labour club in St.Helens."

"Parr and Hardshaw eh. You're nobody until you've played there," laughed Charlie.

"What do you think about the Beatles?" asked Len.

"Not bad. They're nearly as good as us."

"Do you know any of them?" asked Alan.

"Yes. I used to knock about with Stuart Sutcliffe. We were in the same class at school. It was through him I got to know John and Paul."

"Greeno's a big fan of Gerry and the Pacemakers," said Tony. Then he sang out "I Like It, I Like It", rubbed his hands together and said:

171

"Not long now eh kid. That's what he'll be singing soon when he's on his holidays won't it, matey?"

"Why, where's he going? "

"France."

"Yes. But that's only half of it. You ask him who he's going with?"

"It must be a woman."

"You've got it in one."

"Have you seen his girl friend yet? Thelma, the office girl in the Work Study."

"Is that the one with freckles, bit on the short side, mousey coloured hair and nice sexy legs?"

"Yes, that's her".

"No, I haven't seen her."

It was becoming clear to them that their new colleague was going to fit in well. He had kept his head down for the first week, but now his trial period was over. He turned back towards Alan and said:

"I've been to France. I went hitch hiking. It's a great country."

"Did you go on your own?"

"It's the best way."

"What's the farthest you've been?"

"Marseilles. What about you? Have you been there before?"

"Yes, I've been twice. I got as far as San Sebastian last year."

"Did you go on your own?"

"Yes."

"What's your French like?"

"Pas mal. Ca n'est pas une probleme pour moi. Je peux parler Francais tres bien".

"Oh no, you've started him off," moaned Charlie. "We'll never get any peace this afternoon."

"Tell him what that bloke said to you in Bordeaux," said Mick.

Alan said nothing.

"Go on, tell him. We've all heard it a dozen times before. One more time won't hurt us."

"Alright. I'd been travelling about a week, talking French all the time. I was even starting to think in French."

"He normally thinks in gibberish," said Yorky.

Ignoring his comment, Alan went on: "I got a lift with this bloke driving a bread van just outside Bordeaux. After we'd been going about twenty minutes he said to me..."

But before he could say more, Charlie shouted out: "Which part of Belgium do

172

you come from?"

"Well, it's true, that's just what he said."

"What did you tell him? You were the original Brussels sprout?"

"Tell us that tale about that mucky woman," said Tony.

"There's hardly much to tell."

"We'll be the judge of that."

"I was going through this small town right down in the south. It was about two in the afternoon. It was red hot and I was knackered. All I wanted to do was have a lie down so I decided I'd stop there. It looked interesting enough. I walked into the first hotel I saw. There was hardly a soul about, they must all have been having a siesta."

"Or a bit of fun," said Charlie.

"It was too hot for that."

"It's never too hot for that."

"Normally I wouldn't start looking for a place until around five in the afternoon. By that time you can tell which ones to avoid or which ones have got the best looking barmaids. But this day I'd had enough. I walked into the first bar I saw and a woman appeared from behind a net curtain. She was a cross between Anita Ekberg and Tessie O'Shea, wearing a low cut skin-tight dress, a pair of net stockings and bright red shoes. "Oui monsieur," she said with a big smile on her face.

"Je cherche une chambre pour la nuit. Vous en avez une," I said.

"Non monsieur," she said holding her hand out and rubbing her thumb across her fingers, "but I've got one for ten minutes."

"We never did hear what he did next," said Mick.

"I beat it quick. She was awful and she would've probably broke my back."

"The way he played against the Foundry I thought it was broke," said Charlie.

"Which part of France are you going to, Alan?"

"Brittany."

"And are you going to hitch-hike again?"

"Oui, d'accord."

"Do you think they'll get out of Calais?" said Charlie.

"Well, if Thelma shows a leg and he hides behind a bush, they might."

At this point they were interrupted by the arrival of Jack Large and two other draughtsmen from the Mechanical section.

"Eh Jack, do you know this lad? He used to work at your old place."

As it turned out, he didn't, but that didn't stop Jack. Soon he was regaling them with funny stories of things that had happened when he was there. Not suprisingly they were all late back into work.

The next few weeks went by quickly. To enable the shops to complete all the outstanding work, most of the drawings had to be finished, checked and approved by the end of June. Then, during July, the draughtsmen would spend much of their time down on the shop floor helping electricians, wire men, fitters, turners, millers, drillers, sheet metal men, inspectors, chargehands, foremen and everybody else understand exactly what they had drawn.

"So where are you going for your holidays, Stan?" asked Charlie as they gathered round Joan's tea trolley one morning. "Is it Bournemouth again?"

Before he could reply, Tony said:

"Bournemouth, that's just a place for geriatrics. I wouldn't go there if you paid me."

"Les Earnshaw went there and they paid him. He had nearly three weeks there."

"It was Brighton, actually," said Yorky.

"Well, it's all the same place."

"I wonder how he's going on," said Charlie. "Has anyone heard anything about him?"

"You've just reminded me," said Yorky. "I bumped into him last week in town."

"Has he had that book published yet?"

"He never said anything. He was waiting for a bus, so I guess not."

Then John asked Mick where he was going for his holidays.

Before Mick could answer, Charlie said, "He usually goes up on the Alps."

"Very nice," said John innocently.

"The Wigan Alps, that is. He doesn't like to go too far away in case their lad blows the house up."

"What do you mean?"

"Well, the last time Mick went away on holiday, when he came back his shed had been blown all over Platt Bridge. His lad had been in there doing some revising for his Chemistry 'O' level."

"Bloody right. I'm going nowhere. This year he's doing his 'A' levels. Who knows what him and his daft mates will do."

June rolled on into July. By now John, or Riggers as he had come to be called, was fully settled into the electrical section. In fact, sometimes he was the life and the soul of it. He was forever telling them about the band, its activities on the stage and, more particularly, off it. It would appear that the Rainmen had quite a following on Merseyside, mainly young girls who wanted to come back stage and mess about.

And if there was one thing the Rainmen were good at, it was messing about with their female fans. They listened to his tales with a smile on their faces, only half believing what he told them. But it didn't matter if it wasn't all true. He was a good talker and put them all in stitches regularly, except for Stan who was becoming increasingly

174

outspoken about the moral decline of the nation's young people. And then from time to time he told them about Vera who lived next door and whose husband was in the Merchant Navy and totally unaware what a good neighbour his wife had in young John.

John and Alan were now the best of buddies. They had taken to spending part of each day talking to each other in French, much to everybody else's annoyance. John was also going to France during the Works Shutdown. For the first few days he was visiting an old friend in Paris, where he would be made more than welcome in her large flat and small bed. Then it was off to Dijon to another female admirer who lived on a farm along with her equally beautiful twin sister.

Then suddenly on the monday before the Shutdown, he announced that the trip was off. The Rainmen had been given their big chance. They had been asked to play at The Cavern a week on thursday, and it was believed that Brian Epstein was going to be there.

"I'll probably be handing my notice in when we get back off the holidays," he ventured in all seriousness.

"Oh, so there will be something to look forward to?"

"That's right, Charlie. Brian Epstein won't want to bank on The Beatles lasting forever, will he? I'll give them another year at the most."

"What do you think of his band, Greeno?" asked Yorky. "You've heard them. Are they any good?"

Alan nodded. Compared to the Chiselheads, a 1955 skiffle band that used to play in Johnny Shufflebottom's shed in Manor Avenue, the Rainmen were very good. But whether they were in the same league as John, Paul, George and Ringo was quite another matter. But then on the night he had heard them, the acoustics in the Gas and Electric social club hadn't been too good, so it was hard to judge.

"I've written this new song over the weekend. What do you think of it?" And then Riggers sang out, "Two lovers going across the sea, heading on to eternity..."

But before he could go any further, the phone rang. It was Mr. Williams requesting a urgent meeting with the Office Committee later in the afternoon.

"Was that song written about us?"

"Well I had you in mind, Greeno, when I was working on it."

"So if it becomes a hit, do we get ten per cent?"

"I'll certainly give you a signed copy. And I'll tell you what else I'll do for you, just to show I won't forget my friends when I'm rich and famous."

"Don't tell me. Let me guess. You'll leave me your set square and that knackered pair of compasses."

"No. They're going to a museum. The thing is, I was going to go down to Dover in my Uncle Arthur's lorry. He works for a haulage firm in Warrington. So, if you want, you two can go instead. It'a a big cab, so there'll be plenty room, and if you slip him a quid he'll be more than happy to take you."

The rest of the week went slowly by. Len's meeting with Mr. Williams was put off twice. Then, on Wednesday the Managing Director shot off to London to see Basil Wilkinson. Shortly afterwards, rumours began to circulate about big changes. But whatever was going to happen would now have to wait until after the holidays.

Finally Friday arrived and at half past four they all went their seperate ways: Charlie to the bowling greens of Blackpool, John towards possible fame and fortune in Tin Pan Alley, Mick to guard duty in Platt Bridge and Alan and Thelma to the beaches, cafes and hotel bedrooms of Normandy and Brittany.

28

THE HOLIDAY AND THEN A SHOCK

It was not with thirty young men that Alan had been looking forward to spending their first night in France. And it was not with a dozen other passengers in the sick bay of the Youth Hostel in Calais that Thelma would have chosen to enjoy her first night abroad. But due to the fury of the sea that is exactly what happened. It must surely have been the worst summer Channel crossing in years.

She had still not fully recovered on the Sunday morning. It had possibly been made worse by something she had eaten on the journey down from Ashurst. So they spent the day walking round Calais, looking at its market, railway station and shops and sitting in pavement cafes watching the world go by. On Monday morning she said she was alright, but he could tell she wasn't. So they spent the day riding round on the buses, first up to Dunkirk, then over the Belgium border to the town of Furnes, before returning to Dunkirk and back to Calais via St. Omer.

He could tell from the way she ate her breakfast on Tuesday that she was now ready for the road. It was clear that they would not now get as far as Brest, but what did it matter. For Thelma, who had never been abroad before, it had been fascinating just going round one small part of Normandy. They walked to the edge of the town and soon had their first success, a student at the Sorbonne in an old Citroen who took them to Desvres and talked in English the whole way. After that they thumbed for over an hour before three lifts in rapid succession took them into the picturesque town of Abbeville, one hundred and fourteen kilometres south of Calais and their stopping place for the night.

By the time they had found a room in a small hotel near the main square it was turned five o clock. As soon as they had closed the door behind them, Alan flopped on to the bed. Thelma unpacked her ruck sack and headed to the bathroom and to the sound of running water he fell asleep. When he woke there was no sign of her. He looked out of the window and saw her sat below in the sun. He noticed how she caught the eye of the men who walked past. How had John described her, a bit on the short side, freckles, mousey coloured hair and nice sexy legs. It made him feel good to know in whose bed she would be spending the night.

He washed and changed, came down to greet her with a handshake and a kiss on both cheeks, a la Francais, and asked her if she was ready to eat. Thelma nodded. Fully recovered, she was now keen to have her first taste of French food. They soon found a small restaurant and prepared to enjoy the first half of their evening's entertainment. Two hours later they were still there, drinking coffee after having eaten a five course meal and, in Alan's case, having drunk most of a large bottle of red wine as well.

"It seems a long time since I was last sat drinking coffee with you in a place like this."

"You mean Marios on Christmas Eve."

"Oui."

"I bet you can't remember much about it."

"I can. I asked you if you'd any parties to go to and you said you hadn't. I asked you if you would be falling asleep after you'd had your turkey and Christmas pudding, and you said it would have to be something out of a tin because you were hopeless at cooking. And then I asked if all your family were still in Wales, and that was when you told me about being brought up in a home after your mum died."

"I remember watching your face when I said that."

"It really hit me. And when you said you'd just started to read a great book and the time would fly by, as though Christmas was something to get over with as quick as possible, I just had to do what I did. I bet you wish that you'd stayed on that bus now, don't you?"

She smiled and shook her head.

The reason why she would have been on her own over Christmas was that Auntie Lil had gone to stay with her son in Chester, as she always did. On Boxing Day she had had a heart attack and spent the next three months recovering in hospital. And so if Thelma had fallen ill on her own in Grasmere Avenue on Christmas Day, the chances are that no one would have found out until someone like Big Joan, puzzled by her absence from work, had called round. But by then it might have been too late! It hardly bore thinking about.

"And what was the great book you had just started?"

"Well, I hadn't actually started it. It was a Christmas present you see. It was Jack Kerouac's 'On the Road'."

"Who was that from?"

"You won't laugh if I tell you?"

"No."

"You won't tell any one?"

"No."

"It sounds silly now."

"Go on."

"It was from you."

"Me!"

"Yes. Before Christmas, I bought myself a few things I wanted, wrapped them in fancy paper and put labels on them like: To Thelma from Mum and Dad. To Thelma from Auntie Rebecca. To Thelma from Auntie Sarah and Uncle Gareth. And on yours I wrote To Thelma from Alan with Love. Then I put them all in a pillowcase so on Christmas morning I could pretend that I was part of a big family and do what everybody else was doing."

There was nothing he could say to that. It was so sad.

"Don't look so worried Alan," she went on as she took hold of his hands. "It doesn't matter now does it. I don't think I'll have to invent a load of relatives next Christmas, will I?"

They talked again about her first few weeks in Silkstone Street. At the beginning, he had treated her almost as though she was just his little sister. But as he began to see her more and more, he had grown to like her more and more. Finally he realised that he had fallen in love with her. He had started off by doing someone a good turn and he had been well rewarded.

He told her again about what various people at work had said when they had found out about her. He had told her this before but she liked to hear him tell her it again. It was a time when her whole life had been turned upside down and all for the better.

After they had finished their meal they walked round the town before heading back to their hotel room. No one paid any attention to them as they walked into the bar. Most eyes were focussed on a blonde in a short skirt who looked as though she had already been to bed a few times that evening and was more than keen to go again. They went up to their room and looked out of the window at two men shouting at each other in the street below. Then Thelma decided to have another shower while he carried on watching the argument which now involved a young woman and a gendarme.

A few minutes later she reappeared, wrapped in just a towel and ankle socks, and indicated that it was his turn. He took his time enjoying the cool water over his body while anticipating what lay ahead. Then he came back into the bedroom, had a quick look at the now deserted street and then slipped between the sheets.

He had been on the bed with her before but this was the first time he had ever been in one with her. There was never the slightest chance of anything like that happening in Silkstone Street and at home; his mum always seemed to appear at the most awkward moments. He quietly said her name, but there was no response. He edged closer, kissed her on the cheek, but there was still no response. He rubbed his nose against her's and then felt her knee move gently against his.

"I thought you'd gone to sleep?"

"I had. But you've woken me up. I wonder why?"

Then she sat up on her elbows, ran her fingers over his lips and said:

"Alan. Do you know what I'm missing?"

"What?"

"Little Ted"

"Won't I do?"

"Perhaps."

"I'll lie very still and not say a word."

"That's no good. He always tells me a little story before I go to sleep."

"Well, I can do that. What sort of a story would you like?"

Her voice sounded a little husky, almost nervous as she replied.

"I'd like a nice romance with lots of action and a happy ending."

Then she kissed his shoulder and continued:

"And if it's any good, I'll give you what I give him when he's finished his story."

"What's that?"

"A big hug."

"Well that sounds good. Let me think."

Her thigh was now resting against his as she gently stroked his face. There was a brief silence while he thought what to say. His mind had gone blank, or rather there were other things on it as her fingers moved down on to his chest while her knee continued to press against his.

"Go on then, slow coach."

"Once upon a time there were three bears," he finally said.

"You'll have to do better than that, Alan. I want a grown up story. I'm not a little girl now."

He certainly knew that. Ever since she had started eating at Granny's she had started putting on weight, and in all the right places.

"I can't think. Why don't you tell me one? You're good at it."

"You've soon given up. Alright then. What sort of a story would you like? And no falling asleep until I've finished it."

As if.

"How about a romance, with lots of action it, and definitely a happy ending?"

"That's what I asked for."

"I know."

"So you want what I want?"

"Oui."

180

"Alan, do you know what I would really like."

Her hand was now stroking his stomach, while her knee was resting on his thigh and moving slowly higher. He slipped his arm underneath her and discovered she had absolutely nothing on! She moved closer and put her arms around him. Slowly he began and soon the main theme of the story became clear. It was a familiar one, one that would be acted out in bedrooms all over France that night. And as it developed, the juke box in the bar below began to play the latest Charles Aznavour hit record, one by which they would always remember their first night together.

He woke to the sound of a clock striking seven. He lay still, and then heard the sound of running water. She was having another shower! A few minutes later, out of the corner of his eye, he watched her sit in front of the mirror and comb her hair. There was a whiff of perfume as she looked out of the window. Then she walked to the other side of the room, and slipped back into bed.

He felt her hand stroke his shoulder. Slowly it moved down his body and on to the back of his thigh. Then she began to kiss his neck as her other hand began to stroke his head. He counted up to twenty in French and slowly turned over. She put a finger across his lips to indicate that he should not break the silence. He put his other arm out and she slid underneath him.

"Don't make her do anything she doesn't want to do or isn't ready for," he remembered Charlie telling him. But then if she was ready, and she clearly was, then it seemed only right and proper to let Nature take its course. And so for the rest of their time in France, Nature took its course quite often.

They ate their breakfast silently. Anyone seeing them might have thought that they had fallen out. But each time he looked at her she had a mischevious grin on her face. And before finally vacating the room she told him to sit on the chair and look in the mirror. Then she stood behind him and slowly removed all her clothes. Soon they were back on the bed enjoying each other's company to the full. And they hardly noticed when an old French chambermaid, who had no doubt seen it all before, walked into the room and caught them at it again.

The following day they hitched to Rouen, then on through Angers and Rennes up to the coastal resort of St. Quay Portrieux where they spent the weekend. Then they slowly headed east, staying at small and out of the way places, until they finally reached Dieppe in time for the night ferry to Newhaven. Their holiday had started slowly, but as soon as they had left Calais the time flew by. They had thoroughly enjoyed their days meeting interesting characters on the road and passing through parts of France that many of its visitors rarely saw or stopped to explore. And even more they enjoyed their nights, firstly in all manner of bars and restaurants and then in bed together.

But before they knew it, they were back in Ashurst and their holiday was over.

Now it would be a time to tell all the relatives about what they had seen and what they had done, although they would have to miss the best bit out. And at work the rest of them would only want to know whether he had or hadn't and he would just have to hint that he might have.

As soon as they walked into the house, Granny jumped up to greet them. It was as though they had been away for fifteen months, not fifteen days. Within seconds the kettle was on and she was wanting to know how they had got on.

"What was the weather like? How did you get on with all that foreign food? Did you like staying in a hostel every night? Did you hitch-hike? Did you understand the lingo?"

To be honest Granny didn't have a clue what it was like in a foreign country. Grandad did, but then France had changed a quite a bit since he was last there in 1918! Then Thelma produced a present she had bought and to which Granny said she shouldn't have, but was clearly pleased that she had. By now it was time for Alan to go home. They had been travelling a long time and it was work for them both in the morning. Thelma came out with him and on the front step hugged him.

"It's going to be lonely in bed tonight."

"Well, at least you'll have little Ted for company."

"Maybe I have, but he hasn't got what you've got in your trousers."

"Do you fancy going up to Liptrots woods tomorrow night."

She laughed.

"I'll ask Auntie Doris if she wants me to keep an eye on the fish while they're away."

"I hope they're going on a world cruise."

"Anyway Alan, thanks for a great holiday. I really enjoyed myself and I enjoyed being with you all the time and especially at night."

"I know. And so did I. But don't forget our little secret. We stayed in youth hostels."

There was little chance to talk when they all arrived back in work on the following morning. John Barker, the Progress Manager, was buzzing around the office trying to discover why two jobs had not been completed before the Works Shutdown. Everybody clearly had a tale to tell about their holiday and they were all intrigued by the bandage around Mick's head. But they had to wait until their visitor had disappeared to discover the reason.

"Your lad hasn't been trying to blow your shed up again, has he, Mick?"

"If you mean this, Charlie, no. I did it on a nail in the coal house. They had to put ten stitches in it."

"Is that where you've spent your holidays, spying on him and his mates?"

Mick laughed. "He's packed his Chemistry in. He's studying Biology now. And he appears to have got Big Jessica from next door to help him. Anyway, how did you get on at Blackpool?"

"Alright. I won that competition I went in for. I made a fortune. I reckon it must have only cost us a quid for the whole week. And I got my picture in the paper."

Riggers was full of it as well. The Rainmen had played at the Cavern. Brian Epstein had been there and liked what he had heard. Since then they had played at clubs in Runcorn and Southport, and last Saturday had been invited back to Parr and Hardshaw Labour Club, a sure indication that they were now firmly on the road to international musical fame.

Then Tony said to Alan: "Well, did you or didn't you?"

"What?"

"You know," clenching his fist and holding half his arm at ninety degrees to the other half.

"All I'm prepared to say is that I never knew that you could have so much fun without laughing."

"So now you know it's not for stirring your tea with. And what did Thelma think about France?"

"She liked it."

"I bet she did."

But before they could pry deeper, the phone rang for Len. It was from Miss Place telling him to be in the Works Canteen at two along with the rest of the committee for a meeting. Shortly after they heard that all the other unions would be there as well as all the managers and the Staff Association Committee.

During the morning various rumours began to circulate around the factory. Many questions called for urgent answers. Why had Mr. Williams's desk been cleared? Where was he and where were Basil, Norman and Cyril? There was always one of them in the works somewhere. Today they were all absent. And who were the visitors that had been seen in the Rolling Mill during the Works Shutdown by one of the maintenance men?

Finally, all was to be revealed.

At two o clock John Walker, the Personnel Manager, brought to order the sixty or so employees invited to the meeting. He began by telling them that he knew as much or as little as anybody else in the room. Then he waved an envelope in the air and told them that he had just received it by special delivery from London with instructions from Basil Wilkinson to read it out, which he then proceeded to do. It all sounded very mysterious.

"From noon today the ownership of Wilkinson's Engineering Works has passed into the hands of the Miller Engineering and Construction Company of Cleveland, America.

All the existing conditions of employment will remain in force until a longer statement of intent is released in due course. The continued co-operation of the work force is requested and expected in whatever changes may be necessary to ensure the long term future of the new company.

Signed J.T. Wilson Miller
Managing Director*"*

There was much discussion about the issue for the rest of the day. What they had all done over the holidays was temporarily forgotten. What it meant nobody knew. How could they, it had come right out of the blue. The firm had plenty orders and had been in the family for over a hundred years. But with the old man off the scene, Basil was capable of doing anything that suited Basil. And if he could make money by selling off the family firm, well he had just proved that he would do.

A few thought that it might be a a good thing. At least they wouldn't have to put up with Basil Wilkinson or Stephen Williams any more. And then the new owners might bring in some new ideas and be better at running the place. But they were all in for a big shock when on Wednesday, three aged Ivy League boys arrived on the scene and started issuing orders.

And by the end of the week the general view was that they could expect trouble from the Three Stooges. And before the year was out they did!

184